Trains Make U-turns

5 Simple Steps to
Get Your Life on Track

Seth Franklin Sherwood

Dedication

For my mother and father who gave me a childhood of love, fun and hope. They were there to help dust me off after the many falls, setbacks and near train wrecks.

Table of Contents

Chapter 3

*E*nthusiasm:

- FILL UP WITH FIRE FUEL
- ENGINE ENGINE NUMBER NINE
- PRAYER (1of 9)
- MEDITATION (2 of 9)
- LOCOMOTIVE LENSES (3 of 9)
- ADD A BIG Y
- AFFIRMATIONS (4 of 9)
- RE-TRAIN THE BRAIN (5 of 9)
- BODY BOOST (6 of 9)
- DRESS FOR SUCCESS (7 of 9)
- TRAIN TUNES (8 of 9)
- LOCO MOTION (8.5 of 9)
- TIME AND ENERGY MANAGEMENT (9 of 9)
- ROGER THE TRAIN ROBBER
- CALL IN THE TRAIN G.A.N.G.
- NO EXCESS BAGGAGE
- DEPARTURE TIME IS NOW

Chapter 4

*P*hysical Exercise:

- TRAIN THE TRAIN
- MOTION CHANGES EMOTION
- FITNESS FUEL
- MODEL YOUR MENTOR
- THE POWER OF CONNECTION
- BACK TO BASICS WITH BELIEFS

Chapter 5

*O*thers come first:

- A VERY NEW DIRECTION
- THE REVERSE EFFECT
- HAPPY AND USEFUL
- WHOM WILL YOU EMPOWER?
- EVERY CONVERSATION COUNTS

Chapter 6

*T*hankfulness:

- SMILE AND THE WORLD SMILES WITH YOU
- ATTITUDE OF GRATITUDE
- ACTION STEPS

Chapter 7

SUCCESS EXPRESS SUMMARY

- ROCKIN ON THE RAILROAD
- GROW, GROW, GROW
- GOD COMES FIRST
- GO, GO, GO
- TACTICS TO HABITS
- CONTRARY ACTION

Forms and references

Preface

Why the train analogy?

On the Christmas when I was six years old, Santa Claus gave my brother Bradley and me a Lionel model train set. We spent hours and hours in our concrete basement playing with that toy train and tracks, which sat on our warped ping pong table. During the holiday vacation, when we weren't outside sledding, skating or snow fort making, we'd be changing the track or adding different train cars to the authentic looking locomotive. It was almost as big as the one they had on The Addams Family television show. My brother and I had a lot of fun with that train set. It's packed up somewhere in our basement in Amherst, MA. (I say it's mine, he says it's his—maybe after he reads this book he will let me be the majority owner).

"A brother shares childhood memories and grown-up dreams."
~ Author Unknown

When that train was running smoothly around the tracks, I felt happy and peaceful with the rhythmic motion of the train going around and around the metal railway . Sometimes, as adults we forget to experience these joyful and wondrous moments when there's no worry about the past and no stress about the future. Those were the days.

As kids sometimes do, we would put a toy or some type of barrier on the track just to watch the cool collision, resulting in broken parts and pieces strewn all over the green deformed table. We pretended that some cars were loaded with TNT. (I've always liked those explosive initials). Fast forward to my late 20s, I saw this as an analogy to the obstacles on my train track of life, an inevitable train wreck. Back then, I was the one consciously making the choice to place my sister Kaye's Barbie doll on the track. But in my adult life, the problems and difficulties that were being thrown on my track were placed there by someone else. It couldn't possibly have been me, could it? Was it the work of God? Was it Karma? I had some serious questions. All I knew was that my freight train was headed for a crash and I wasn't sure who or what would survive the impact.

"Just because you have life, doesn't mean you're living it." ~ *Author Unknown*

Sometimes this idea of a major train wreck in my life sounded like an easy way out of the depressing, bare and purposeless life I was living. My life was deliberately wasting away. Now keep in mind, I do not consider myself to be a big train buff. But the idea that my life was an out-of-control freight train loaded with TNT is a powerful metaphor. Many clichés have been used to describe the meaning of life—Life is like a box of chocolates, a round of golf, a baseball game, a marathon, a mouse looking for his lost cheese—but to me, life is like a train trip. We are either enthusiastically advancing to a definite destination with intention, purpose and ambition or we are taking a boring ride to Nowhere Land, perhaps struggling to a certain degree or even experiencing excruciating emotional pain as we trudge in the muck and mire of life.

"Failure is a detour, not a dead-end street." ~ *Zig Ziglar*

Unlike most trains, this train—my train, YOUR train-- can make a U-turn. It might involve laying some new tracks, or re-training the current engineer, who is you. But it can be done, and I can gratefully say that I have done it and I'm still enjoying the ride. I am applying the principles outlined in this book and achieving fantastic results. I am still a work in progress. This is a lifelong endeavor. It is not a do it once and then you're done.

"In order to succeed you must fail, so that you know what not to do the next time." ~ Anthony D'Angelo

You cannot transmit something you don't have. I cannot write about climbing Mt. Everest because I have no experience in doing that. What I do have experience in is hitting bottom, causing a near train wreck and then finally undergoing a complete transformation. My purpose in writing this book is to pass this message along to others. I am just the messenger keeping it simple. If it works for you, great. Many friends and acquaintances over the years have told me they were never given the "How to Live Life" manual. This book will hopefully serve as one of those "Life 101" instruction manuals. My intention is that the tactics in this book will help you as they have helped me. Of course the tactics have to be implemented. They must be applied and re-applied with all the fortitude, courage and determination you can muster. We need to make them part of who we are. Practice makes permanent. This might seem daunting at first, but it actually gets easier the more you practice. It is like learning to ride a bike, pretty simple after a while. Simple, but not easy.

"Repetition makes the master." ~ Author Unknown

Introduction

The year was 1987. I was 29 years old and had recently relocated from Massachusetts to Long Beach, CA. My Aunt Carmen allowed me to stay with her until I got on my feet with a decent job and place to live. I believed that California was the land of milk and honey and that my past misfortunes would be behind me, way behind me. Time for a new life...didn't happen. I had traveled 3000 miles across the country to leave my problems back East and begin a new life. However, it's like they say, wherever you go, there you are. I was still struggling with things like stress, worry, irritability, anger and absolutely no direction in life. For most of my life I used alcohol to numb these feelings of despair, self pity and inadequacy. The beers, scotch and tequila had worked for years and now for some reason, the anesthetized effects of those spirited libations had deserted me. I frequently felt angst and impending doom. ARGH.

"I try to be a truthful artist and I try to show a level of courage. I enjoy that. I'm a messenger." ~ Jeff Koons

Two years later I made a major decision which completely turned my life around. This resolution and the subsequent consistent action steps have put my life on a path of joy, adventure and excitement. Do I still have any stress, worry, irritability, anger or lack of purpose and direction in my life? Seldom, very seldom. When those first thoughts and subsequent negative emotions invade my mind, I now use the tactics delineated in this book. They allow me to quickly and effectively get back on track without alcohol or band-aid treatments. I've learned it's an inside job. Most of the time, I live a life of freedom, joy and growth with definite direction in my life. Some might call it a miracle, and I would wholeheartedly agree. You might be at a point in your life where you have some very important choices to make too. Does your train have a destination or is it a heap of metal just struggling and putt putting along, barely getting by day by day? Do you want to merely survive or would you like to thrive? I wrote this book to help people get off that rotten railroad ride and jump aboard a new powerful train, the Success Express.

"One decision can change your life around in a very astounding way ." ~ Bill Johnson

As the saying goes..."to keep something, you have to *give* it away." My aim is to share these train tactics with you. Your train can also make a U-turn. A friend asked me if I was "*giving*" the book away. Not exactly. The question is, who wants to make an investment which can result in a HUGE payout. My train has made a Gigantic U-turn and I know where I'm headed. The journey I am on is simply fantastic. I wake up with joy, excitement and a spirit of adventure. Follow these steps and you can achieve similar results. Ben Franklin said, "An investment in knowledge pays the best interest."

KEEP IT SIMPLE

I have created a simple way to remember the five train tactics to a joyful, purposeful and enthusiastic journey. These five principles are listed below: (or above)

- **D** irection
- **E** nthusiasm
- **P** hysical Health
- **O** thers First
- **T** hankfulness

"Make everything as simple as possible, but not simpler." ~ Albert Einstein

DEPOT, as in train depot, I think you'll agree, is an easy acronym to remember. Making it easy to recall is important. There are so many other things to remember on a day-to-day basis that this simple word reminds us of these very valuable life-changing principles. Many of us need reminders. It's so easy to get caught up in toxic things like the rotten economy, terrorist threats, murder trials and just overdosing on television.

Remembering the acronym is the easy part, putting it into practice can be a challenge. If it were easy to make these changes, I wouldn't have written this step by step detailed guide on how to enjoy your non-stop journey on the Success Express.

Can trains really make U-turns?

"If we don't change, we don't grow. If we don't grow, we are not really living." ~ Author Unknown

"It takes courage to grow up and be who you really are." ~ E.E. Cummings

Chapter 1
Train Wreck or Success Express

"The greatest discovery of any generation
is that a human being can alter his life
by altering his attitude." ~ **William James**

THE LOUSY LOCOMOTIVE

Are you the engineer of a Lunky Lousy Locomotive?
Your day doesn't start out the way you want. Even
before you get out of bed, the conductor in your head is
yelling out, "Next stop, Worry Warehouse, after that—
Self-pity Platform"

*"Thoughts are boomerangs returning with precision to their
source. Choose wisely which ones you throw." ~ Anonymous*

Do any of these thoughts ever enter your mind when
you wake up or even during the day?
* My financial situation won't improve, and will
  even get worse
* The things people have said or done to me are
  causing my misery and terrible circumstances.
  (blame, complain and self-inflicting pain)
* How will I handle my needy kids, my lousy job,
  the house and car repairs, the lack of money,
  declining health and my nagging spouse?
  (Overwhelmed with life)
* My significant other doesn't appreciate me, or
  even worse, no one does. (maybe just my mom)
* There's no such thing as gravity, this world
  just sucks...

9

If and when these types of thoughts enter your mind and you don't make a prompt proper adjustment, you might be headed for derailment. Perhaps a minor annoyance starts your lousy-locomotive down the same destructive path. Maybe the ironing board was left too close to your tracks on your commute to the bathroom. The shower takes too long to heat up. The shirt you wanted to wear has fallen off its hanger and is now a wrinkled mess on the floor of the closet. You sweat the small stuff. Your train is off track and a train wreck might lie around the bend.

"Success is how high you bounce when you hit rock bottom." ~ George Patton

WHO ARE THESE CAREFREE CABOOSE CHARACTERS?

I have always been suspicious of people who seem to have a genuine, positive attitude. I used to think to myself, *"I'm existing in this perpetual state of doom and gloom, can't these people leave me alone and stop smiling so much? How can they possibly be so happy, day-in and day-out?"* It seems impossible to maintain a positive, hopeful and cheerful attitude every single day. Your mind gets bombarded by thoughts about financial failure, rotten romance, gas prices, poor health, international conflicts, family problems, spousal dissatisfaction, hot weather, cold weather, shoppers with 15 items in the 12 item or less line, incompetent drivers. It's the pits. One of life's greatest challenges is to walk around with a seemingly carefree perspective that everything is fine the way it is, and that in the end it will all work out just splendidly.

These people seem to do life on life's terms. How do they do it? Many of them apply the same principles discussed in this book. Now you can also be happy, joyous and free. Just stay on track...

TERRIBLE TRAIN WRECK

Back in the late 90s on a beautiful sunny Southern California day in Long Beach, I was playing catch with a friend of mine, Ron. We were throwing a nerf football back and forth to each other. The little physical exercise I was getting seemed to be relieving me of some anxiety and stress. Perhaps I was going to make it through this feeling of impending doom. I then decided to stop playing catch with Ron and said, "That's enough, I'm going inside." Before I got into my apartment, he threw the ball once more and it hit me on the upper right hand frame of my glasses. They got bent a little. I got bent a lot. I reacted or rather overreacted. I let the F-bombs fly with the fire and fury of a raging bull. Then I turned to the huge mirror hanging on the side entrance door. I kicked it with all my might and the glass shattered into thousands of pieces. There was a big crashing sound and Ron rushed over to see what had happened. I turned to him and angrily shouted," I told you not to throw the f-ing ball." He turned, looked at me in the eyes and said, "Whoa."

"People who fly into a rage always make a bad landing." ~ Will Rogers

After that incident, I realized that there was still a festering ball of stress, anxiety and rage in me. I was a walking time bomb ready to explode any second. Maybe

11

some physical exercise would do me some good, but perhaps I needed something more. A few other similar experiences like that occurred over the next few months. The pain and angst got worse. It was very real. I would look at myself in the mirror when I was shaving and saw an evil image looking back. Me evil? I thought I was a nice guy. What happened? Why can't I just calm down? Why can't I have any peace?

"If you get upset when the toast burns, what are you going to do when your house burns down?" ~ Author Unknown

Maybe my rage was a learned behavior. In many instances it was the only way I knew how to deal with a difficult situation. *I remember when I was about six, shopping at JC Penny with my father and brother. My dad just wanted to buy a toaster. We were in the home appliance department and not a single sales person came to help us. After a few minutes, my dad lost his temper. He yelled out so the whole store could hear, " Is there anyone in this F...ing place who can help me buy a F...ing toaster? Within 10 seconds three JC Penny people came running to the home appliance department. My father looked at them and calmly said, "Thank you, I'd like to buy a toaster." Wow, I guess that's how you get things done.* Just scream at the top of your lungs, with profanity and rage. So, was it learned behavior or did I have the "rage" reaction in my genes? Don't know. I do know that I have screamed at the top of my lungs many, many times, with many, many, swear words. That, I learned as an adult, is inappropriate behavior. Besides, throwing temper tantrums was not working... at all.

I later realized what it meant to hit rock bottom. I couldn't stand myself. The complete feeling of despair, exasperation and HELL! I felt completely trapped and pinned down; I wanted to scream as loud as I could at the world "Life sucks! And MY LIFE REALLY, REALLY SUCKS!!!" I desperately needed something new, something better, something to change this crappy feeling that hovered over me constantly like a dark cloud. I wanted new fuel for my locomotive, a new engine, and a new load of cargo to haul every day. I needed to change. I couldn't stand myself (I said that already). Do other people go through this kind of anguish and despair?

"Only God can turn a mess into a message." ~ Anonymous

Then, one day, I heard a wise train conductor say, "if nothing changes, nothing changes" and "if you keep doing what you're doing, you'll keep getting what you're getting." I'm not sure if this is what one would call an epiphany, but I realized I needed to change my attitude —this fatal feeling, this sickly stench that seemed to envelop everything in my life. I asked myself, "Is that a simple thing to do, change my attitude?" I wasn't sure. What I did know was that my old ways and methods weren't working, and the last thing I wanted was to continue this miserable life. I felt like a grumpy old man and I was only in my late 20s. I needed to change the track I was on and transform my lousy locomotive into a high-speed bullet-train that would take me somewhere away from me. Sometimes I felt like peeling my skin off so I could get down to the raw pain of living. There was also a part of me that truly only wanted some peace. Just some calm, relaxing peace. I had no peace, none whatsoever. Gimme some gosh darn cotton pickin f -ing peace! And give it to me NOW! I didn't even know what real peace was. Just ugly RAW feelings of angst.

CAUSES OF RAILCAR CHAOS

The other day I heard the following message on my friend Larry's answering machine: "Hey, I hope you're having a wonderful day, and if you're not, then it's your fault." It was blunt and to the point. What a blessing it was to get that message. A single sentence recorded on a voicemail was all it took for me to take control of my thoughts and change my attitude for the rest of the day; I was able to have my train make a U-turn. Sometimes we need simple reminders that we are the ones who make the choice of how to direct our thoughts and attitudes. Could your train use a change in direction?

"A problem clearly stated is a problem half-solved." ~ *Dorothea Brande*

A teacher writes the following equation on the board.

$$\frac{2}{2}$$

She then asks the class, "What is the answer to this problem?" A few students respond "4", one says, "0" , but most of the class sits and waits to hear the answer. The teacher then explains that there is no answer because of the fact that we don't know what the problem is. First things first. The instructor states that the sign (+, -, ×, or ÷) needs to be determined.

14

"Pain is the touchstone for spiritual growth." ~ Anonymous

12 step programs use this concept as well. The first step to finding the solution is knowing the problem. Many people don't like to admit they have a problem. Who does? Who likes to admit they are weak, defeated and/ or unsuccessful? People will think we're **LOSERS**. Our self-image, self- esteem and self-confidence might be destroyed, annihilated and crushed to little bitty pieces, OUCH! This starting place is crucial. Just like reading a map, it is impossible to get somewhere if you don't know where you are. This bottom is where we start our action steps and then it's the *do, do, do, the dah, dah, dah.* (Sorry, still stuck in the 80's music).

ALL ABOARD THE SUCCESS EXPRESS

Shovel in the coal and fire up your train's engine. Leave Stench Station behind. Use these tactics to re-chart your course and put yourself on track with an awesome attitude and an intentional life. Living a life with intention is one filled with joy, excitement and expectancy. You control all of the buttons, keys, levers, knobs and switches on your locomotive. You are in full command of your engine. Although, you're not alone. You will be harnessing a omnipotent power whose purpose is to help you on your train ride. You will soon wake up every morning with PASSION!!! A passion to live life to the fullest. You will live life and you will love life. Stay on track...

This is your journey, your exciting and adventurous trip to the destination you choose. Let's get on board and ride this train together. It's more fun and prosperous when we ride with our friends. We laugh and learn from our mistakes. We support each other and celebrate our successes. We make better decisions on our trip. We grow. We become leaders in our families and communities. Our trip depends on three things:

1. Having a crystal clear destination of where you are going. Living an intentional life. (Chapter 2)
2. Igniting your ENTHUSIASM by applying these powerful train tactics. (chapters 3-6)
3. Enjoying your journey with an attitude of Adventure Excitement and Joy.

Maybe trains can make U-turns...

"Habits are like train tracks, they take a long time to put into place. Once they are there they will take you anywhere you want to go."
~ Patricia Fripp

Get on track, stay on track, and don't look back

Chapter 2

Depot

Direction

"Efforts and courage are not enough
without purpose and direction."
~ **John F. Kennedy**

This is where it all begins. Do you have a vision of
where you want to be in three, five, or ten years from
now? You need to have a target, a destination. As the
song from the South Pacific musical goes, "you gotta
have a dream to make a dream come true." So where
and how do you find your direction, your dream, your
vision? Here's what happened to me.

*"If you don't know where you're going, you'll end up someplace
else." ~ Yogi Berra*

One Sunday morning maybe 15 years ago, I attended a
church service near my home. Rick Warren gave a talk
on something called "A Purpose Driven Life."
Apparently, I was at the point in my life where I was
ready to hear that message. It was the ole *"when the
student is ready the teacher will appear."* Pastor Rick
said that God gives us all a purpose for being here on
Earth. Our job is to find out what that purpose is and
then do the best we can to make it happen. This
purpose is what your inner voice, your intuition, your
heart, your higher power, or God directs you toward.
This source can be a bit mysterious. But let's keep it
simple so as not to delay our train's departure.

"Without the assistance of that Divine Being ... I cannot succeed. With that assistance, I cannot fail." ~ Abraham Lincoln

POSITIVE POWER PLATFORM

Each of us has a choice to believe or not believe in this entity that many call God. There are self-proclaimed atheists who believe that God does not exist. There are agnostics who play it safe. They believe it's impossible to know whether there is a God. I do know that it's a good idea to be open to the many different spiritual concepts and beliefs. It is of course completely up to the individual to decide what he believes about God and then what he calls this being.

"We can never know God is all we need until God is all we've got." ~ Author Unknown

In the late 90s, I turned my life and will over to the care of God. And that's when my train started making a U-turn. It works for me, it can work for you. Call your higher power whatever you feel comfortable with. Some examples include the following:

- God
- Higher Power
- Allah
- Jesus
- Inner Voice or Inner Being
- The Law of Attraction or The Universe
- Name you choose _____

One person I know calls his "prayer meeting" his Higher

Power. When he attends the meeting, he believes God speaks through the participants in the group. To start your spiritual journey, it's important not to get hung up on the name. Remember the Lao Tzu saying, "the journey of a thousand miles must begin with the first step." If this is too big a step for you to take right now, keep reading and stay on board. Don't ever jump off a moving train. It works in the movies, not in real life.

"None of us will ever accomplish anything excellent or commanding except when he listens to this whisper which is heard by him alone." ~ Ralph Waldo Emerson

I choose to call him God. I like simple. He is Numero Uno in my book. When I think of how He has transformed me from a destructive diablo into a lively laughing locomotive, I'll continue to make my personal relationship with God the most important part of my life. God allows me to have a freedom to enjoy life, to enthusiastically chase my dreams and to delight in a peace which passeth all understanding. My relationship with God has also given me the gift of loving myself. I had a huge challenge with self-loathing, feelings of inadequacy and train loads of fear. You can't heal a sick mind with a sick mind.

Some people I know use the "fake it till you make it" technique. They take the action and get on their knees and pray, even though they are not 100%, 50% or even 1% sure there is a God. Heck, even Mother Teresa had doubts about God. A co-worker once told me that there is "so much we know that just ain't so." I've had my doubts too. From the time I began to turn my life and will over to the care of God, little by little, my faith has grown and keeps growing. For some people it happens quickly, for others slowly. My spiritual growth has been S   L   O   W   ...very slow.

"Do not ask the Lord to guide your footsteps if you are not wiling to move your feet." ~ Author Unknown

I had a huge challenge getting on my knees and praying. *Years ago, I was at our home in Long Beach, CA. The kids and I were watching TV. I then felt a subtle nudge. The idea I had was for me to get on my knees and pray. Well, I didn't want to pray in front of the kids, as that might indicate I was a weakling. So I went upstairs to the bedroom. I closed the door and walked over to the bed. Before I got on my knees I thought I heard someone coming up the stairs. I opened the door to check where the kids were. Nothing. They were all still downstairs watching TV. Returning to the side of the bed I kneeled down to begin praying. Again, "was there a noise outside the door?" I checked...nothing.*

*Finally, I quickly got back down on my knees and prayed. It went something like this: "God, I don't know if you can hear me. I know you're busy. But if you have a few spare moments, would you please give me a hand and help me with this impending feeling of doom, this worry and anxiety that I just can't shake? That's all for now God. I'd really appreciate a quick response." I quickly jumped to my feet for fear my kids would see a fragile father. What were the results? I remember that I felt a subtle, very subtle sense of relief knowing that my worries were in God's hands, not mine. Things have worked out...*they always do. Without really understanding it, my train continued making its U-turn.

If you have already begun your journey with your Higher Power, fantastic. Remember, He is the director. In chapter two we will discuss how to develop and maintain this powerful partnership. For now let's focus on one thing... asking Him for direction.

"I have an unshakable faith that comes and goes." ~ Bob S.

After hearing Pastor Rick's message I regularly prayed something like this:

Me: (on my knees) "God, Thank you for all the help you've given me. Please keep guiding me and helping me in all areas of my life. I'm guessing I might be one of your biggest challenges, but you are God. So I know you can do it. Now I've got another favor. Would you please somehow tell me what my life's purpose is? I think you want me to enjoy life, use my talents and gifts to the best of my ability and help others. I just need some specifics. You know like 'What career should I pursue?' I'd like to have some nice toys too. Is that being selfish? I mean I'm willing to share my toys. Most of them. But how will I make my millions in order to buy all these cool things? Anyway, I know you're busy. I'll be back and in the meantime thanks again for the peace of mind I've experienced lately. I actually feel more at ease with myself. You're good God, I mean that too. You know what you're doing so I'll leave it all up to you. Talk later. Oh yeah, I've got some very cool ideas on how to make the big bucks. Next time maybe..."

God works in mysterious ways. That I know for sure. How will he work in your life? Good question. Embrace the mystery. Just keep asking Him in your thoughts as frequently and as focused as possible. If you've never done this before and you meet up with a friend you haven't seen in a while your conversation might go something like this:

> **You**: Hey buddy, how you been, what's new?
>
> **Friend**: Pretty good, just hangin' in there. You know same, ole, same ole. What's new with you?
>
> **You**: Well I've been asking God what my life's purpose is. Just asking for some guidance. It's a new thing, thought I'd try it.
>
> **Friend**: Really? Wow, let me know if it works. I've been floundering for the last sixteen years. No direction, no purpose, paying bills and just kind of existing and getting by, but I think maybe I gotta do something different.
>
> **You**: Yeah well, don't tell anybody. But if it works, I'll let you know. Who knows, next time you see me I might be a totally different person.

DON'T DELAY DEPARTURE

One question which I was asked more than a few times when I tentatively joined my first prayer group was, "is your way of doing things working?" And I had to regularly and realistically reply, "no". But did I want to move forward with this God thing? Not really. Although I understood the point my new friends were making. I guess I wanted something visible, tangible, some kind of sign. I needed proof. How can you prove something that you can't see? "Try it," they said, and "keep coming back." Yeah right, nice tag line, NOT. Let's look at things from a more logical perspective. What does research indicate are the best reasons for living a God centered purposeful life? I found pretty much equal backing on both sides. That age old debate between science and God still exists. So, all I've got is my personal experience. Works for me...

Your decision to live an intentional life guided by God doesn't have to come right this instant. But consider it and do your own research. Be open and willing...
Look at the table below and you decide

Living an intentional life "ON TRACK"	Not living an intentional life "OFF TRACK"
You develop and maintain a deep feeling of value and self-worth	Not living up to your full potential, a feeling of lacking something
Having definite direction and a sense of where you are going	Uncertainty in some big decisions and small ones as well
Being challenged in various areas of your life so that you grow to your fullest potential	Little or no significant growth in areas of knowledge, skills and emotional intelligence (attitude)
Growing in the most important area of your life, relationships	Not developing and enhancing your life through relationships
Having FUN, enjoying activities like singing, dancing, sports and other interactive events	Not enjoying the richness of connecting with friends and family in fun activities, (boredom)
Living a life with an attitude of AD- VENTURE, JOY and ENTHUSIASM!!!	Stressed out, you allow little things and big things to get to you (i.e. drama queen)
Improved health with vim, vigor & vitality: **mind, body** and **spirit** are in alignment. Living & **LOVING** life	Increased probability of sickness, injury, or other poor health symptoms. Stress=dis-ease

Living a life of intention seems like a no-brainer to me. Some of you might be thinking, "show me the money." Ah ha, glad you asked or thought about that. My experience has taught me that spiritual development has to come first. You can make some big buck-a-roos with a good business plan, Effort (with a capital E) and persistent action but... why work harder than you have to when you have the Chief Engineer (you with God's guidance) running the show? Don't you think it makes more sense to partner with Him? Again, your Higher Power will guide you, direct you, and make sure you grow in the process. Expect Him to help you. Expect Him to always be with you. Expect a miracle. That's what He does...miracles.

"Every time you don't follow your inner guidance, you feel a loss of energy, loss of power, a sense of spiritual deadness." ~ Shaki Gawain

PURPOSE #1

What is my purpose? My primary purpose is threefold: 1. To improve my personal relationship with God. 2. To do his will. And 3. To be happy, joyous and free. Seems pretty simple. Remember I do not claim to be a spiritual, serene, pious saint or Godly guru. My way of life just did not work for over 30 years. Irritable and discontent are two words that I use to accurately describe my regular state of mind and emotion. Pretty much a miserable existence. There were some fun events and memorable experiences. Overall though, I did not like myself...at all. Now, I do my best to lead a God centered life. One's primary purpose is sometimes called your "awakening". For me, I need to take the time and make the effort to talk and listen to God. It's a life-long process. I turn everything over to God. That means decisions and plans about relationships, career, finances, health, little things and big things. I believe God gave us all brains to use. I can make sound decisions... not that I always do. We all make mistakes. But as Dr. Phil says, "Sometimes you make the right decision, and sometimes you make the decision right." I regularly ask myself, am I truly living a God centered life? Am I doing right now what God would want me to do? I think he wants me to write this book, so the answer for the moment is "yes". It also helps to remember that I am not perfect, I am not a saint and that God wants me to grow. It's progress, not perfection. My mom used to say, "we can always do better."

"There are three stages in the work of God: impossible, difficult, done." ~ James Hudson Taylor

PURPOSE #2

My secondary purpose is something different. It's more of a "doing" thing like a career or a mission, and it can also change over the years. As I stated before, I believe God wants us to enjoy life to its fullest and to use our gifts, passions and strengths to help others. That being said, all I have to figure out is what would make me feel joyous and enthusiastic if I were to do it on a full-time basis. (How about eating chips and salsa while lying on the couch watching ESPN all day?) Joseph Campbell said, "follow your bliss". What does that mean Joe? Just go for self-gratification all day long?

"Life is either a daring adventure or nothing." ~ Hellen Keller

GET ON TRACK WITH GPS

You might have a Global Positioning System in your car or phone. It is, as you know, a map that gives you directions on how to get from point A to point B. Your new U-turn train **GPS** is about your **G**ifts, **P**assions and **S**trengths. When you get to page 29 take a moment to write what your **GPS** s are in the spaces provided. Think about some of the activities you loved doing and I mean REALLY loved doing when you were a kid. Maybe you loved cooking, building things or gardening. Take some time and try to remember those childhood playtimes.

"The purpose of life is a life of purpose." ~ Robert Byrne

When I was about 12 years old I regularly practiced my Ibanez acoustic guitar in the living room of our house back in Amherst, MA. I simultaneously blew into my $5. harmonica, held in its metal holder around my neck, (à la Bob Dylan). For hours I would teach myself a Roy Clark tune from "Roy's Popular Music Songbook". Once I had sufficiently practiced a song, I would walk down the hall and enter my mother's room. I'd say, "Okay, I think I have this one down. Listen and tell me what you think." Every time I played a song for her she'd say, "Yeah, that's good Sethy, that's a good song. Keep practicing." I left the room with a bigger smile, a lighter walk and ready to learn a new song. Ahhhh, those were fun times.

"When you are clear, what you want will show up in your life, and only to the extent you are clear." ~ Janet Attwood

During high school and college, I occasionally played guitar with my friend, Andy Smith. We would perform for the neighbors from my apartment balcony. Many times about a dozen kids around would come and sit on the grassy slope. They'd watch us play some rock and roll songs and we'd pretend we were big time rock stars performing at Madison Square Garden. Great fun memories. I've jammed with other guitar players while overseas in the Peace Corps, in France when I was visiting some friends and in California. Basically almost anywhere I can pick up a guitar and play. It has always been a favorite pastime of mine. Just plain fun. It's part of who I am.

" My guitar is not a thing. It is an extension of myself. It is who I am." ~ Joan Jett

What are my gifts, passions and strengths? I thoroughly enjoy entertaining an audience. Just like my dad used to do. I Love the interaction, the laughs and the connecting with the crowd.

Look at three of my GPS s I have written on the next page. Then come up with your own GPS s. Remember, think of some of the most enjoyable childhood experiences you had. Turn off the television, get a pen and some paper and just start jotting down what those experiences were. Later on you can dig deeper and see what you come up with. Meditation has helped me tremendously get more clarity of my vision. Being still and quiet can significantly help pinpoint your destination.

"Your work is to discover your GPS and then with all your heart, give yourself to it." ~ Dr. Sheth

27

I love to enthusiastically sing and play my guitar. I play rock and roll, blues, easy listening, folk songs and ballads. I also like to improvise and create some fun lyrics. Keeping it fun is huge. Music is a big part of my life. It helps improve my attitude on a regular basis. I created and produced two bilingual children's music CDs. Performing in front of a live audience is Funtastic!

Maybe I got this passion and now a strength from my father. He thoroughly enjoyed making people laugh by telling jokes or reciting LOL lines in a musical comedy.
After a 16 year stint as a school teacher I have embarked on a career which allows me to deliver engaging and energizing keynote speeches to empower audiences of all ages.

Each year Toastmasters runs two speech contests, These competitions bring out the best in the participant. Writing, delivering and competing in these speech contests has motivated me to continuously work on improving my speaking skills.

Now it's your turn: draw or attach a picture of what you really enjoy doing; your gifts, passions and strengths. Then write about them on the right side.

My secondary purpose is the following: **to engage and inspire individuals and groups of people to do their best, be their best and live and work with 10 times more ENTHUSIASM.** Before your train moves forward, do your absolute best to discover what your primary and secondary purposes are. Your train needs a destination. This is why we start with "D", for Direction. The real benefit is the sense of peace, reassurance and purpose I've received from my growing faith in God. Even the word "priceless" does not come anywhere near to describing the gifts I've received as a result of my personal relationship with God. Get on track, stay on track and don't look back. This is your NEW Life!!!

"When the voice on the inside becomes more profound, clear and loud than the voice on the outside...then you've mastered your life." ~ John Demartini.

STAY ON TARGETED TRACK

You have (or soon will have) your direction, your passionate purpose, and you're starting to lead an intentional life. You basically know what you gotta do, so do it. Well, it's not that easy. Time for a plan? That's coming. Enjoy the feeling of knowing you are now "on track". Many people are not on any kind of track, are off track, get side tracked or are even on the wrong track. Some people get on track, but they don't stay on track or even worse, get derailed. How can we avoid that? How can we trek forward on our track?

To stay on track we need to focus. One of the most effective methods of developing and maintaining focus is to "visualize" (discussed in more depth in chapter 3).

I continue to practice and improve this train tactic on a daily basis.

"When you decide clearly and definitely what you want, then no sacrifice is too great as you put all of your powers into astounding results." ~ Charles Allan

On a regular basis, I visualize scenarios focusing on my various visions I have created. Here's my picture story...

I am in Budapest, Hungary. I am sitting at a café with a friend of mine. This is my second time here in Budapest in the last two years. Each time in this marvelous country I make a few good friends. These new friends are very kind and generous. They take me out to various restaurants, cafes, museums, and other special places which are both interesting and a huge pleasure to visit. My friend's name is Omar. He is giving me a brief history lesson on Hungary. I thoroughly enjoy learning about the history and culture of this fascinating country.

I am eating a Kifli (a crescent shaped cookie, made with butter, pecans, cinnamon sugar and a yeast raised dough). I take short sips of my delicious Hungarian egg coffee. While Omar goes inside the café to buy himself another beverage, I sit back and look at the old street this store is part of. It is dreamlike. There are other cafes, shops, old buildings, people walking around and some kids riding their bicycles. It's almost unbelievable that I am living my dream of keynote speaking all around the world. I think back to how this whole thing started. How I left my 16 year teaching career to pursue a different path. I relied completely on my personal relationship with God...which I still do.

31

Before Omar comes back, I look in my man purse (I am in Europe) and take out my passport. I open my passport and look at the different colored international stamps from all the different countries I have visited in the last three years. The countries include, France, Spain, Italy, England, Germany, Greece, Turkey, Russia, India, Chile, Ecuador, Argentina, Hungary, Egypt, Kenya, Slovenia, Japan, Portugal, Guatemala, Peru, Switzerland, Costa Rica, Honduras, Mexico, Iceland, South Africa, China, Canada, Brazil, and Venezuela. I take another bite of my Kilfi and then sip my rich coffee. Ahhhhh...

Later that day, I head back to my luxurious hotel. I am in the business center and I check my email and then Facebook. I enjoy the inspirational quotes some friends have posted. Always good to get those reminders. I post a few photos from my trip including a picture of a Kilfi and tell my family and friends what's happening in this fantastic world of abundance, joy and freedom. Life is good...all is well. Thank you God. I am blessed.

"I would visualize things coming to me. Visualization works if you work hard. You can't just visualize and go eat a sandwich."
~ Jim Carrey

RAILROAD RISK

Back in 2004 I was teaching English at a high school in Orange County. I had been a schoolteacher for over 14 years. The first seven were in elementary school, grades 3-5. Now I taught ninth grade English. The kids were fun and most of them had a pretty good attitude.

One morning I was erasing the blackboard at the back of

the room. The students hadn't come in yet and the classroom was quiet and still. As my right hand with the eraser in it made a swipe across the board I felt a sudden awareness that I wasn't alone in the room. I turned around to see if a student had entered, but no one was there. I made a few more swipes and then felt the same presence I had experienced a moment earlier. Again I turned and the room was empty and quiet. What was that I wondered. It reminded me of one of those misty spray bottles you use during the summer to cool down. Like someone had sprayed me with this mist. And while it wasn't water over my whole body, something almost tangible was nudging me. Again, I thought, what could it be?

"You have to leave the city of your comfort and go into the wilderness of your intuition. What you'll discover will be wonderful. What you'll discover is yourself." ~ Alan Alda

Let's rewind the tape a bit. For the 6-9 months leading up to that auspicious day in my classroom I would regularly entertain thoughts of leaving my teaching career. What type of career would I pursue? I didn't know. That experience at the blackboard seemed to give me a push to think about my options. Should I leave teaching? I was a tenured teacher. My salary was pretty good with 15 years of teaching and a graduate degree. Plus teaching is a fantastic career. It comes with tons of intrinsic rewards. Seeing the light bulb go off in a child's head when he/she understands the lesson is a very cool thing.

"All life is a chance. So take it! The person who goes furthest is the one who is willing to do and dare." ~ Dale Carnegie

Yet there was something saying to me, go for it. Make the career change. Chase your dream. Use your God given talents to the best of your ability. At the end of the school year when the secretary asked me to sign a letter of intent which stated that I would be returning the following year, I checked the box that said... ☑ no.

If your life is ever going to get better, you'll have to take risks. There is simply no way you can grow without taking chances." ~ David Viscott

Was that a risk I took? More than a few people have told me my decision was stupid, dumb, crazy, immature and idiotic. My future ex-wife almost decapitated me when I told her of my drastic move. But I look back on that defining moment of my life with absolutely no regrets. I felt a sense of Freedom. I would pursue my dreams with all the passion, persistence and power I had. But this was all new ground. I had taught American history in the elementary grades and I remember reading and studying the pioneers who came out West. Those people certainly took huge risks. They risked their lives for something they were not at all sure about. Would those early American pioneers find a better life out west or would they die at the hands of indians, disease or severe weather conditions? Was I a trailblazer or a turkey? Yes, some people thought they heard me gobble gobble. I was heading out to uncharted territory.

"When you discover your mission, you will feel its demand. It will fill you with enthusiasm and a burning desire to get to work on it." ~ W. Clement Stone

Leaving a 15 year teaching career for what? No idea. But I knew God was with me. Let's just say I really hoped He was with me. Was God guiding me? This next story played a key role in my life changing decision.

THE WRONG TRACK

Back in 1989 I started my career as an elementary school teacher in Norwalk, CA. There was a veteran teacher who befriended me. His name was Don. At the start of the year, Don pulled me aside after lunch one day with a serious look on his face. I felt a bit uncomfortable. He then asked me, "Seth, what are you doing in teaching? Why did you choose this career?" I wasn't sure what he was getting at. I told him the truth. I replied that I enjoyed working with kids and that it seemed like a good career. I added that my father was a teacher and he seemed to take great pleasure in educating young minds. For the next 15 minutes Don told me how the teaching profession was the worst possible career to pursue. He had a long list of compelling complaints and nasty notions of teaching. Not a fun conversation. I finally asked him why he hadn't left teaching. He said when he was around 28 his mother got sick and he needed a steady job to pay the hospital bills. Teaching was his only work experience since college. After a few years of job security and a decent income he felt trapped with no career choices. Listening to Don's story made me think. I vowed to escape from any job or career if I ever felt I trapped or imprisoned like Don. I am not proud to say that my excessive drinking, years ago, resulted in being arrested and locked up for DUI and protective custody. I remember the bleak feeling the morning after when I came to. Not just the hangover. I felt the gloom of being behind bars, captured, and lifeless. It sucked. I followed through on that commitment. It's been years since I've felt imprisoned, both in jail or in my real life. We have choices. No big regrets like Don had, not for this engineer. Life is about joy, growth and freedom. Freedom to make choices.

This book is about my experiences in finally growing up. If your **GPS**, calling, or secondary purpose is to teach, then by all means teach. The world needs inspirational, passionate teachers. Strong role models who ignite a student's fire for making the most out of his or her life are in short supply. I applaud all the teachers who are making a difference in this world.

I think trains can make U-turns...

"The person who risks nothing, does nothing, has nothing, is nothing, and becomes nothing. He may avoid suffering and sorrow, but he simply cannot learn, feel, change, grow or love.
Chained by his certitude, he is a slave; he has forfeited his freedom. Only the person who risks is truly free." ~
Leo Buscaglia

Back to the DEPOT

D.E.P.O.T. **D**irection, do you know where you're going?

Chapter 3

dEpot

Enthusiasm

"Nothing great was ever achieved
without enthusiasm." ~ **Ralph Waldo Emerson**

FILL UP WITH FIRE FUEL

Your train is on its track and you know your
destination. Now it's time to get your motor runnin
(head out on the highway, lookin for adventure, in
whatever comes our way). Love those old Steppenwolf
lyrics. What was the name of that song? Born to Be
Wild. Wild it is. Here's how. Your engine needs fuel. Top
quality, 1st class, high test fuel. Or else. Or else your
train is stuck at the stagnant station. Your fuel is
ENTHUSIASM. 10 Xs ENTHUSIASM. Remember what
Ralph said, "nothing great was **EVER** achieved without
enthusiasm." You have a great purpose right? A great
vision too? You now need an attitude of 10 X s
ENTHUSIASM!!

*"Catch on fire with enthusiasm and others will come for miles
to watch you burn." ~ John Wesley*

The source of the word "enthusiasm" is the Greek
enthousiasmos, which ultimately comes from the
adjective *entheos*, "having the god within". He guided us
in our search for our purpose and now He'll lead us to
achieve the best possible attitude. It takes more than
just a carefree positive attitude to stay on track and get

to our destination. The question many ask is "how do I go from feeling doubtful, indecisive or even only a little hopeful to a 10 Xs Enthusiastic feeling?" Let's start at the beginning, and hold on mama, it's ROCKIN ON THE RAILROAD time!!!

ENGINE ENGINE NUMBER NINE

The first choices you make when you get out of bed in the morning, frequently determine how your engine will run for the rest of the day. Will it sputter along, putt, putt, putt? Or will your locomotive leave the station with passion, power and purpose? You choose.

"The most powerful weapon on earth
is the human soul on fire." ~ Ferdinand Foch

The nine steps below are what I do to start my day. These early morning fire fuel steps are what sets up your success. Engine Engine Number 9 is an old song recorded by Roger Miller in 1965. At Crocker Farm Elementary School when we had to decide who would be up first in a game of kickball, the ole Engine Engine Number 9 decision making process was used. Let's look at these 9 fire-fuel train tactics and see how they can turn traditional train fuel into a powerful propellant.

PRAYER (1 of 9)

We discussed this in the last chapter. As I mentioned earlier, my personal relationship with God is my number one priority. The most important thing I can say about prayer is "try it". A friend of mine throws his keys under his bed every night before he goes to sleep. When he wakes up in the morning, he knows he needs his keys. While he's down on his knees retrieving his keys, he says his prayers. That works for him. As you read earlier, my prayers are a regular conversation with God.

"Prayer is exhaling the spirit of man and inhaling the spirit of God." ~ Edwin Keith

There are a handful of prayers which I do slowly recite every morning. I start my day with prayer, end my day with prayer. (and I pray during the day too). I Thessalonians 5:17 says "pray without ceasing." Love that. Most of my prayers include appreciation, requesting guidance and I do ask God to help those who are going through challenging times. That means people, animals, and specific situations. These are personal requests and I end with, "thy will be done". Pretty simple.

MEDITATION (2 of 9)

The key is to have an open mind and be willing. I encourage you to research meditation for yourself. Friends have told me that prayer is talking to God and meditation is listening. Start out being still and quiet for five minutes every morning. Give it a shot for 30 consecutive days.

Back around 1990 I was attending a regular Sunday morning prayer meeting at the Marina Pacifica in Long Beach, CA. About 12 of us met from 7:00 to 8:00. One day after the meeting a friend from the group asked if I would like to join him and some others at his house for a meditation meeting. I had never meditated before. I wasn't sure how to respond. I did trust this man. He was one of the leaders of the prayer meeting and everyone seemed to look up to him. His name was Chris and he frequently quoted famous authors such as Mark Twain, Emmett Fox, Joseph Campbell and many others. I ended up saying yes. I got directions and drove to his house.

"I follow the RPM method every morning. Rise, Pee and Meditate." ~ Janet Ong

Walking up the driveway, I noticed about seven other cars there. This wasn't going to be a small group. Maybe 10-12 people. I said hi to a few friends I knew from the 7:00 A.M. prayer meeting. After chit chatting for a few minutes, we all moved into the family room. There were three very comfortable looking armchairs, a sofa and some people had brought their cushions, pillows, yoga mats etc...Everyone got comfortable in their meditation space. I sat in an armchair. Then Chris passed a few books around for people to read out loud. These were meditation books based on teachings from Christianity, Buddhism, Hinduism and some general readings on the benefits of quieting the mind. I just sat there and absorbed what was happening. This was all very new to me. I questioned myself. Is it a good idea to meditate with these people who I didn't know very well?

It was too late to run and never come back. So I stayed put, listened to the readings and watched the other meditation members. More doubt and fear crept in. My mind wandered. I know this is a spiritual exercise but I felt confused and questioned if I was going to be hurt in

40

some way. Then it happened. The readings had finished and Chris grabbed his timer. It was time to meditate. He sat on the floor and said, "time to zone out, see you all in 20 minutes." He turned the timer on and that was it. Quiet. Stillness. Space. Nothing. Weird.

"No great work has ever been produced except after a long interval of still and musing meditation." ~ Walter Bagehot

Just complete quiet. No one was talking, moving, or fidgeting. Now my mind raced more than ever. "What was I doing here? Are these people crazy? Do these people really stay still and quiet for the whole 20 minutes? I think I'll open my eyes and peek to see if everyone is really meditating. What if one of them has a knife? Or what if they're taking off their clothes to perform some kind of sick cult sacrifice? What if it's me they're going to sacrifice? They'll probably cut my jugular . Love that word, "jugular", rhymes with "juggler" I think. Well kind of. I shouldn't have come. Why did I come here to meditate? These people are crazy. No one can sit still and be quiet for 20 minutes.

They're up to something. Did I pay that electric bill on time? That chick with the sexy blue blouse and nice cleavage likes me, I think. What was her name? Sharon, Sandy, I think. Yeah Sandy. She talked to me. She asked me how long I'd been meditating. Is she single? Should I talk to her after this weird meditation thing is over? I'll have to act all spiritual and mature. Can I do that? Can I act mature? Sometimes I act mature. Mostly though, girlfriends, wives, everyone else sez I act immature. Crap. When am I going to grow up? I loved those fluffer-nutters mom used to make. Fluffer-nutters, no one eats fluffer-nutters any more. It's fun just saying

41

fluffer-nutter. How can anyone eat creamy style peanut butter? You gotta eat extra-crunchy.

Is the 20 minutes almost up? How much longer? What's that smell? I'm hungry. I love that song I heard on the radio, Steely Dan's "Reelin in the Years." Brings back memories of Amherst. Those were fun times. I wonder if my mom threw away my hockey skates. She always throws my things away without asking. Why does she do that?

"All prosperity begins in the mind and is dependent only upon the full use of our creative imagination." ~ Ruth Ross

Those were just some of the thoughts I had when I first meditated. Yes my friends, quieting the mind has been no easy task for me. Now, I can better control the thoughts that enter my mind. My mantra, "Be still and know that I am God" helps a lot. When I meditate I can usually be completely still and quiet for 5-10 seconds. I also slowly recite the prayer of Saint Francis of Assisi. Start with five minutes of meditation and then lengthen it to 10, and finally 30. I follow an 8 step program which suggests 30 minutes in the morning and 30 at night too. Choose a mantra and stick with it. Be still and listen. Remember, the same letters that are in 'LISTEN' are also in 'SILENT'.

The main benefits from meditation include the following:

1. Greater sense of peace and direction throughout the day. I don't usually react to situations. I pause and then respond. (most of the time)
2. Increased creativity in personal and professional challenges.

3. Greater ability to stay focused in the moment.

"A wise man will be master of his mind, a fool will be its slave."
~ Author Unknown

LOCOMOTIVE LENSES (3 of 9)

We briefly discussed visualization in the sub-chapter called <u>Stay on Targeted Track.</u> This tactic is so important that it needs to be examined a second time. Many very successful professionals credit visualization to effectively achieving their vision.

Olympic athletes—gymnasts for example, spend large amounts of time visualizing themselves performing perfect routines before it's their turn to execute in front of the judges.

Research has revealed that the subconscious mind cannot tell the difference between what is real and what is imagined. This means that when you think of images of what you desire, and truly believe that you have achieved or acquired those desires, the vibration/ energy that you emit (your feelings) attracts similar energy in the form of opportunities and ideas to manifest those images. It's like driving to the park. You see it happening and you expect to arrive at the park and play wiffle ball. And poof, it happens. You can do that with your deep down desires. So imagine, visualize with clarity and believe in your dreams. And take ACTION!

"Vision without action is merely a dream. Action without vision just passes the time. Vision with action can change the world."
~ Joel Barker

ADD A BIG Y

One key element to making the most of visualization and getting on the right track begins with the "WHY". That's right, you must have a big enough "WHY" in order to maximize your visualization and reach your destination. When you ask yourself, why do I want to be successful? What is your answer? Is it just to prove to a parent or an ex-spouse that you can achieve success despite what they think? You can achieve your vision that way although you might not truly enjoy your railway ride. Remember, God gave each of us gifts, passions and strengths. How are you using those? Your why has to be BIG enough so the drive and determination will get you to your destination. It's adding that necessary ingredient of "emotion". It helps to find out what your "core" values are. God? Family? Your legacy?

"You must find the place inside yourself where nothing is impossible." ~ Deepak Chopra

Imagine that your house is burning. Trapped inside is your son, daughter or someone very close to you. The fire fighters are not there and you are the only who can crash through the door to save your loved one. You're not going to think about hurting your shoulder or even losing your life. Your number 1 concern is saving her life. Nothing else matters. Take that same level of intensity and apply it to your vision. Focus on it, believe you can do it, believe you are doing it. Make it an obsession. You have other responsibilities like your family, your health, your finances etc...Take care of those too.

When you're not engaged in any of those other activities, work on your vision. Action, Action, Action. Think how achieving your vision will have an extremely positive effect on those other areas of your life. Do it for God, do it for you, do it for your family. Just do it.

I would not bet against you accomplishing it. You know why? Because you have a HUGE WHY!! With this kind of leverage, you will act differently...you won't put things off, you won't fear rejection, you won't care what other people think about you, you won't sit around acting confused and telling yourself you just don't know why you can't get motivated. You will take the action and GET THINGS DONE!!! It's like a fire. If your fire starts to dwindle, add some "WHY" fuel and get those flames flying high and WHY-ILD. It's Rockin Railroad time!

"To change one's life; Start immediately. Do it flamboyantly. No exceptions." ~ William James

A very important aspect of this idea is repetition. All of these tactics require taking the action over and over again. We want to build up the memory and feelings of how to be successful. The more you repeat the visualization the clearer it becomes and the stronger the feelings are. It's **DAILY DEDICATED DETERMINATION!**

AFFIRMATIONS (4 of 9)

Affirmations are statements of goals and visions you desire, written as if they were already accomplished, with an emotion added. If the goal is time-sensitive, set a date. Say your affirmations out loud first thing each morning, in the afternoon and last thing each night.

> *"Whatever you put into your mind - in one way or another - is what you will get back out - in one way or another."* ~ *Shad Helmstetter*

Many quantum physicists believe that by adding a powerful enthusiastic emotion to your affirmation you create and send out a high frequency vibration which attracts similar vibrations. (just like visualizations) These returning vibrations include creative ideas which, when acted upon, can help manifest our affirmations. Yes, we need to act on our visualizations and affirmations. Did I say that already? Hmm, must be important.

Here are a few of my examples and visuals I use:

- I am enjoying spending time with my family. **Image**: We are at a family reunion in Amherst, MA, having a barbecue in the backyard, throwing the frisbee and kicking the soccer ball.
- I am a successful professional keynote speaker. **Image**: I am at the Vistalegre in Madrid, engaging and inspiring 12,000 enthralled attendees.
- I am joyfully sharing my abundant wealth with my family and friends on fun things like travel, family entertainment and sports. **Image**: my family and I enjoying shrimp cocktail in first class seating en route to Spain.
- I am in a fulfilling, fun and intimate relationship with my significant other. (Working on **Image**)
- I'm in tip top shape. I weigh 185 lbs, have six pack abs and a 32" waist. **Image**: scale at 185 lbs., six pack abs, and wearing 32" waist slacks.

Create your own affirmations and use powerful language, vivid images and make them in the present tense. Think **BIG**. You are the one creating expectations for yourself. Now it's your turn. On the lines below write down at least three affirmations. Remember to:

• Keep it in the present tense, start with "I am…"
• Keep it positive
• Be clear and specific
• Add powerful images to your affirmations

1._____
2._____
3._____
4._____
5._____

Repeat these affirmations aloud throughout the day. Visualization goes hand-in-hand with affirmations. Add positive emotion as best you can and finish with the phrase, "I am blessed."

> *"Successful people do what unsuccessful people are not willing to do." ~ Anonymous*

Let's review where we are before we proceed. Here's my daily routine up to # 4:

1. Wake up at around 5:30 AM. Hit my knees and pray. Turn my life and will over to His care. Hydrate by drinking a glass of water and splashing some cool H20 on my face. Healthy and refreshing.
2. Sit in the lotus position for 30 minutes of still time which includes: **prayer, meditation, visualization,** and **affirmations**.

3. After meditation it's time for a rich cup of java. One cup limit. Used to do three and got over caffeined out. Whoa big fella, slow down...
4. Next I turn on my ipad, click on my reading material and begin to **re-train my brain.** Stay on board.

"The secret of your future is hidden in your daily routine." ~ Mike Murdock

RE-TRAIN THE BRAIN (5 of 9)

You've heard the saying, you are what you eat. If you were to eat a greasy burger, shake and fries every day, you'd probably get big and fat. The mind works the same way. If we watch or listen to negative news, violent crime shows and decadent programs, our minds will absorb those images and messages and produce similar thoughts, feelings and possibly actions which are not in alignment with our purpose, vision and goals. Remember this: GIGO = Garbage In: Garbage Out.

So instead of feeding our mind with destructive debris, which leads us to a railroad wreck, let's feed it with high test fuel, which will power our engine with Energy and Enthusiasm. Here's what I do in step 5. I read two to three pages from a handful of inspirational books. I highlight the most meaningful passages and phrases.

"Books can be dangerous. The best ones should be labeled 'This could change your life.' " ~ Helen Exley

I peruse these books many times over. A friend of mine told me that he's read "How to Win Friends and Influence People" 60 times. We read inspirational books, repeatedly apply the prosperous principles, they become habits, and these habits make up our character. That leads to our success. You BECOME a more successful person.

"The more you read, the more things you will know. The more that you learn, the more places you'll go." ~ Dr. Seuss

When my mind takes in prayer, meditation, visualization, affirmations and inspirational readings it becomes a turbo-charged, highly energized engine. Notice there is no television, radio, emails, Facebook or anything from the external world. Remember, it's an inside job. Like the roots of a tree. The fruits depend on how healthy the roots are. We are changing unhealthy habits to success habits. Before entering the arena, you are warming up to bring your "A" game. Let's move on to the second part of Engine Engine Number 9.

BODY BOOST (6 of 9)

We have covered the spirit and mind in the first five tactics. Now let's incorporate the body. We want the body, mind and spirit to all work together harmoniously. While chapter 4 focuses on the **Physical Health** component in much greater depth, light early morning health boosters are an effective train tactic to energize our engine. You may decide to get an early morning strenuous aerobic/ strength training workout or just some light exercise, stretching or Yoga to get the blood flowing. How much time and effort you dedicate to your physical health in the early morning depends on your work and or family schedule. My work schedule varies from day to day so I plan my vigorous daily workouts (6 per week) on Sunday night.

> *"He who has health, has hope; and he who has hope, has everything." ~ Thomas Carlyle*

As I stated earlier, you are what you eat. Plan your meals in advance. Make sure you are consuming enough vitamins and nutrients to power your engine. When I Googled "books on nutrition" I got 163,000,000 results. Follow a healthy regimen either from a credible book or a nutritionist/doctor. I am constantly looking at new and different ways to eat smarter and reach my maximum physical health potential.

In chapter 4 we will discuss the how aligning our physical health with our thinking and spiritual dimension is crucial to riding our train in a state of joy, adventure and enthusiasm!

DRESS FOR SUCCESS (7of 9)

My mother used to tell my brother, sister and me, "Appearance counts." It has taken me a very long time to grasp and apply those words of wisdom. Appearance does count. I admit, my mother still sends me nice shirts, slacks, ties and vests. She really pushes the importance of always looking your best. As many mothers do, she reminds me to be clean and floss daily.

> *"Your dress is a part of your attitude. If you dress like you are successful, it will make it easier for you to act like you are successful, in turn making it easier to become successful." ~ Lia*

I have slowly learned to always look my best. No, I don't

wear a tuxedo to the gym. But I don't wear a ratty old t-shirt, faded out socks and tattered shorts either. If I want to be a professional, I have to look like a professional. That means I must dress the part.

A few months ago I was walking up some stairs at an office building with my friend Annette, who was about a step or two behind me. When we arrived at the top of the stairs she turned to me and said, " Do you mind if I tell you something a little personal?" "No, I don't mind." I replied. " Well your jeans don't fit, they make you look cheap and sloppy. Is that what you want?" She quipped. Wow! No one had ever told me I looked sloppy. (Well, maybe my mother.) Later she told me about designer jeans. And that I should invest in getting a pair or two of top quality, fashionable and close-fitting jeans. Well, the next day I ordered a pair of Calvin Kleins online. They came in the mail eight days later. Yes, they are close-fitting and a few people have actually commented on how slender I look. I do think I look better and consequently feel more self-confident. Thank you Annette.

Who would want to board a train that looked defective and damaged? Your train not only needs to have a high

"How things look on the outside of us depends on how things are on the inside of us." ~ Author Unknown

performance engine, it needs to look sleek, stylish and snappy. The point? Appearance counts. Wear clothes that are of good quality, in fashion and fit well. One of the ways people judge us is on how we look. So always do your best to look sharp. This means with our physique, our hygiene and the clothes we wear.

All of these nine fire-fuel train tactics are powerful. This next one is not only powerful, it's FUN! **Listen to vibrant vivacious music**. Let's look at the power of music. Research shows that music is the single largest facilitator for creating happy thoughts. Music can not only calm your nerves but it can actually motivate a person to execute beyond their normal performance level. This has been observed in athletes, artists and sales people. Music affects a steep rise in the levels of serotonin, which has positive influences on brain cells controlling mood.

"Music gives a soul to the universe, wings to the mind, flight to the imagination, and life to everything." ~ Plato

As I'm doing my daily hygienic duties and getting dressed, it's railroad rock and roll time. I'm brushing my teeth and mufflingly singing along to Van Halen's "Jump". The playlist labeled " ENERGIZE " is a favorite. It includes rock and roll from the 60's to the 90's. This train tactic as mentioned above is FUN. You MUST have fun on your train ride. A big part of success is enjoying the journey and making the most of each moment. Music helps me to squash indecision, doubts and fears and just have fun where I am, whoever is there, and at that moment. So sing, whistle or hum a merry melody.

"I don't sing because I'm happy, I'm happy because I sing." ~ William James

When I go on a run or workout at the gym, I exercise with my ipod cranking out my "SUPER ROCK" songs. These tunes are not the kind you would listen to when you're trying to set a romantic mood. No sir ree Bob, they'll be no lovey-dovey, honey-bunny here. These songs are booming, blaring and blasting. We're talking about bands like The Kinks, the Cars, and Queen. You'll get ignited by that concert of turbo-charged tunes. Feel the music. Let it go deep inside you and feed that fire of purpose and passion. During an invigorating workout session with the train tunes cranking, my endorphins are flying around like bees gone bonkers. It's a high! I'm psyched, and set to conquer the world! It's showtime baby! Get your motor runnin! Music is POWER! Harness that POWER! Be that POWER!

LOCO MOTION (8.5 of 9)

Some people dance to celebrate, to attract a mate, to bond socially and some just do it because it feels right. Do you like to dance? You will. Research shows that exercise makes you happy. Dancing is exercising. Hence dancing makes you happy. Some people say, "you gotta dance when the spirit says dance." And I say "dance and the spirit will spring and sparkle." So boogie down, hop, twist, salsa, merengue, cumbia, or even line dance...whatever. Just move your feet, arms, hands and hips. Have fun. Studies shows that dancing increases self-confidence. Dance in the bathroom, dance in the kitchen, in the driveway, the parking lot, the office. Sing and dance. Dance and sing. Throw in some fist pumps. Try a double fist pump. Oooh Yaozza, Yaozza, YAOZZA!!

"There is a bit of insanity in dancing that does everybody a great deal of good." ~ Edwin Denby

TIME AND ENERGY MANAGEMENT (9 of 9)

Are you changing? Are you growing? Are you starting to feel that fire in our belly that today is the BEST DAY EVER? It will come...trust the train. And now the gran finale of the fire-fuel train tactics . Drum roll please dadadada. Thee...... **Daily Action Plan**! That's right. Your engine is all revved up. Now we have to make sure we are on the right track. Otherwise, we are like that toy train my brother and I used to play with. It was fun to watch, but it just went around in circles...forever. No destination.

There is a saying in the military and business world. "Proper Planning Prevents Painfully Poor Performance". It also goes along with the "It's not that people plan to fail, it's that they fail to plan." Can I say it anymore clearly? Plan, plan plan. When? Before your day starts. That means the night before or the Sunday night before the work week begins. If you're like me you might think, well I like to shoot the from hip, I can wing it. I'll just go with the flow and do whatever inspiration comes to me.

"Action is the real measure of intelligence." ~ Napoleon Hill

As your train's engineer you need to know what stops to make, what tracks to switch to and where to re-fuel if necessary. Set your daily, weekly, and monthly goals. What is on your "to do" list for tomorrow? What time will you accomplish them? You can't manage what don't measure. Set goals and evaluate how you did. Then make the proper adjustments. Set the bar high and work hard. Follow the TRAIN technique to goal setting and achieving.

Besides organizing your day before it begins, think about what time during the day you have the most energy. Let's say you are a morning person. Schedule the activity which requires the most creativity, interpersonal focus or definite one-pointed attention in this time slot. Mine is from 8:00 AM to 11:00 AM.

Another success tip is to write the five most important things that will get you closer to achieving your goals. Write them down from one to five in order of importance. When you start your work day, tackle item #1. When

TRAIN technique to goal setting and achieving:

T enacity. Be tenacious. Remember all we covered on the first 8 steps to maintaining that 10 Xs ENTHUSIASM attitude? Now add tenacity. You now have tenacious enthusiasm. We're talking Determination, Perseverance and Commitment.

R esults oriented. This means that we need a target to aim at. How many calls, emails, appointments, laps, pounds...something measurable & specific. A goal that anyone can tell if you achieved it or not at the end of a definite time period.

A chievable. Make sure when you set your goal that it is a target you can hit. Don't set your goal too high or you may feel discouraged if you don't achieve it. You can start out low one week or month and after you've hit it, then raise the bar the following week.

I n the zone. You will reach a point where you are performing with all cylinders firing at maximum capacity. Not only is your Enthusiasm high, you are fully focused. Believe you will reach this dynamic dimension. Many professional athletes and performers get in this "ZONE".

N ew and Nutty ideas. Always be looking for ways to improve the process. Keep that question in the back of your mind, " What would be a more effective way of reaching my goal(s)? When I say "nutty" I mean be creative and innovative. Try something different. Make sure it's legal though. Think outside the tracks.

that one is completed, go to the next one and then further on down the line. Simple or simple?

"Don't wait. The time will never be just right." ~ Napoleon Hill

The idea is that when we achieve our goals, we gain more confidence, we take time to celebrate our success and recognize that we get closer and closer to achieving our vision. We then really start to feel like our Train is on Track. Nothing can stop this Powerful Locomotive.

"The great aim of education is not knowledge, but action." ~ Herbert Spencer

For almost three years I really didn't have a definite goal for completing this book. I just knew that eventually I'd get it done but...hey no pressure, no biggie, no rush. And guess what? I got side-tracked, off track and even back-tracked. The book project got stuck, stale, and stagnant. (okay enough alliterations) Here's what happened. First I made my relationship with God my number one priority (got some definite direction). Then I improved my attitude with the Engine, Engine Number 9 train tactics. After that I realized that beyond a shadow of a doubt, I would achieve my vision. (I came to believe). Applying the TRAIN goals and especially making them achievable and measurable was a huge help. I AM Tenacious, in the zone and always looking for New and Nutty ideas to work more effectively. Will achieving this goal get me closer to my vision of being an international keynote speaker, coach and author? Yes. A big YES! A GIGANTIC YES!!!

"Inaction breeds doubt and fear. Action breeds confidence and courage. If you want to conquer fear, do not sit home and think about it. Go out and get busy." ~ Dale Carnegie

ROGER THE TRAIN ROBBER

We have now covered all Engine Engine Number 9 train tactics. Not everyone gets the same results. Some people can reach and stay in the 10 Xs ENTHUSIASM zone for up to five or more continuous hours. It's like they've drunk six expressos and nine Red Bulls. I like to be able to choose throughout my day which level of Enthusiasm is best for whatever task I am tackling. Some presentations I give might be most effective when I am at my highest level of enthusiasm. Others, maybe not.

Then there is that 2-12% of indecision, doubt and fear which we must be aware of and not allow it to exterminate our enthusiasm. It can stifle our growth, kill our dreams and even cause a fatal train wreck. I have named this killer. He is called Roger the Train Robber.

"It takes but one positive thought when given a chance to survive and thrive, to overpower an entire army of negative thoughts." ~ Robert Schuller

Roger's secret mission is to sabotage your trip. Beware, for Roger is a subtle foe. He can cleverly trick us into believing that he is our true inner voice, our real self, our protector. Roger has caused thousands of train wrecks, maybe more. You must first recognize that he will do whatever it takes to get you off track. He is a murderous mind mole. Roger inflates the indecision, develops the doubt and feeds the fear. Oh he's a sly, devilish, evil robber he is. What is the best solution? Two answers: Solution **A**, go back over the Engine Engine Number nine fire-fuel tactics. Or go to solution **B**; call in the **Train GANG**. This is the short version of Engine Engine Number 9. Simple and effective.

CALL IN THE TRAIN G.A.N.G.

A while back my significant other told me that our relationship was over. Yes, my feelings were hurt. Poor me, poor me, poor me. What could I do? I guess practice acceptance. But I didn't do that. I let it fester in me and allowed it to poison my thoughts 24/7. Then I finally remembered that those thoughts were shrewdly being cultivated by Roger the Train Robber. I then called in the Train **GANG**. Here's solution B.

G: Pray to **God**. Talk to God. He's listening. Sometimes he watches us grow. God is there with you. Trust Him.

A: Take **Action**. What action can you take to move you closer to achieving your goals or helping others? Focus on your vision and goals. Motion changes Emotion.

N: Stay in the **Now**. Focus 100% on what you're doing at that moment. Do the very best you can in whatever activity you're involved in.

G: Make a **Gratitude** list. Thank God that you're breathing, walking, seeing, etc...keep repeating "thank you God, thank you God, thank you God...

That, my friends is the **TRAIN GANG**. Call 'em in and remove Roger the Train Robber before he poisons your passion and ruins your railroad ride.

58

NO EXCESS BAGGAGE

Before we leave the station we need to make sure we're not carrying any excess baggage to weigh us down. What do I mean by excess baggage?

"Few things are as powerful as an honest, sincere apology." ~ Author Unknown

Back in my early 20s I was engaged to marry a lovely lady named Alice (not her real name). My partying, drinking, and very immature behavior produced some very hurtful words and actions from my end. One of my blunders was to run out on Alice, my three month pregnant fiancé. One morning at the condo her father had bought us, after I had been on a two day bender with a friend of mine, she told me I drank too much. How dare she. After she left for work, I packed up my bags and loaded my blue 1982 Toyota Corolla with my priceless possessions. My Ibanez acoustic guitar, a laundry basket full of dirty undies, books, Yonex tennis racquet, Penn balls, and a six pack of Bud, (I paid for it. It was mine.) I found a yellow post-it pad. Ripped off a single sheet and wrote these four simple words," wedding's off, good luck." I slapped it on the frig. I showed her. No one tells me I drink too much. Then I drove to my father's place and told him what I had done. He was familiar with my unpredictable and bizarre behavior so it didn't shock him whatsoever.

After finally getting sober, and doing my best to reconcile my past blunders, I learned that I might still be carrying some guilt (excess baggage). This guilt, along with other past harms also known as freedom blockers, had to be thrown off my train.

In 1992 I went back to New England to visit my mother, brother and sister and their families. A big part of this trip was to make amends to Alice. We talked on the phone. I told her I was sorry for abandoning her to have the baby. She didn't forgive me. In fact she asked how I could live with myself after the way I had treated her. Wow, I wasn't prepared for that. Later that week I met with Father Quigley of the Newman Center at UMass. He told me that I didn't need her forgiveness. If I had made an honest and sincere apology for my hurtful actions, that I could then move on and that the situation was closed. I did my part. Making amends allows me to regain not only the trust and respect of others, but more importantly the trust and respect I have for myself. My train was now really ready to take off with no excess baggage holding me back. YAWWWW...HOOOOO!!!

"A man should never be ashamed to own he has been in the wrong, which is but saying... that he is wiser today than he was yesterday." ~ Alexander Pope

I ask God to forgive me for my transgressions. He does. I forgive myself for the harm I have caused others and all my wrong doings. You must get rid of any excess baggage before your train leaves the station. Professional help is sometimes necessary to heal and move forward. This forgiveness step is very liberating and can make the difference between a joyful journey and a troubling, trembling trip.

The child who I ran out on was born October 24, 1986. Amanda is her name. She is a professional model, dancer and actor. Although I have not met her face to face, we have corresponded by emails, holiday cards and Facebook. I hope to meet her and make a more personal amends. That is all in God's hands, in God's timing. A mantra that works for me is; I can't, He can, I think I'll let Him.

"There is absolutely nothing that gives a person more satisfaction than knowing they're on their way to achieving their vision." ~ David Schwartz

DEPARTURE TIME IS NOW

We have determined our purpose and direction. We have the Engine Engine Number 9 Fire-Fuel train tactics to power our dynamic departure. Adapt them to what works best for you. If during the course of the day you think Roger the Robber is nearby, call in the Train GANG. I frequently crank the "Energize" tunes when my Enthusiasm level starts to diminish. Staying connected with God through prayer and meditation is huge. Practice visualizations in the afternoon, and some inspirational readings too. These tactics work like a spring board to get powered up and pointed in the right direction. Practice them every day. You cannot stay warm on yesterday's fire. Even if you don't FEEL like doing them, DO them anyway. Keep your head, hands and heart on track. Do your best to STAY ON TRACK.

"In order to live life you must love life and in order to love life you must live life." ~ Author Unlknown

1. Prayer
2. Meditation
3. Visualization
4. Affirmations
5. Re-train the Brain
6. Body Boost
7. Dress for Success
8. Train Tunes
8.5. Loco-Motion
9. Time MGT/ Energy

Trains CAN make U-turns...

Get your motor runnin...

"The key to success is to raise your energy; when you do, people will naturally be attracted to you. And when they show up, bill'em." ~ Stuart Wilde

Back to the DEPOT

D.**E**.P.O.T. **E**nthusiasm, start your day with the Engine, Engine number 9 FIRE-FUEL tactics.

Chapter 4

DE**P**OT

P hysical Health

"If the body be feeble, the mind will not be strong."
~ **Thomas Jefferson**

Your direction is clear, your focus is improving, and there is power in that. You are now controlling your thoughts and emotions. That's the Fire Fuel to give you Fantastic Force. You will soon understand that in order for you to keep the Success Express running at its peak performance, you'll need your physical being to be firm and fit. Just like any other machine, vehicle or piece of equipment, our train needs to be in tip top running condition. If an engine doesn't get a tune-up, adjustment and proper maintenance, it runs the risk of faltering, failing or falling behind schedule.

"Those who think they have no time for healthy eating, or exercise, will sooner or later have to find time for illness." ~ *Edward Stanley*

Our body needs this same type of maintenance. In the first three chapters we discussed our spiritual, mental, and emotional states. Do you remember the sixth early morning train tactic for achieving 10 Xs Enthusiasm? That's right, it's the Body Boost. Even though it's good to get the blood flowing in the morning, our train requires more than a quick jump start. We're talking a high performance mean, lean mighty machine. Let's look at the importance and benefits of keeping our physical bodies in outstanding, exceptional shape. Our physical condition will now mirror the growth we make in our spiritual, mental and emotional development. Just like the previous two chapters it's all about taking intentional action. This chapter on physical health requires mucho movement. If you're not ready, do it anyway. Wait a minute, I am NOT a doctor. (Don't even play one on TV.) Do not start a physical fitness program without getting professional advice from your doctor or health expert. My lawyers told me to write that in.

"It is exercise alone that supports the spirits, and keeps the mind in vigor." ~ Marcus Cicero

Besides helping to fulfill our primary and secondary purposes, by achieving and maintaining outstanding health, the chances increase that you'll get to spend more time in your golden years with your grandchildren, grand nieces and nephews or great grandchildren. Or you can travel around the world 17 times. Or sky dive at 99 years young. Remember Spock's words of wisdom, "live long and prosper." My version is "live long, prosper and have a BLAST!!!" I use a lot of exclamation marks don't I? I'm the author, I say it's okay. In fact, let's change that. I say, IT"S FANTASTIC!!!

TRAIN THE TRAIN

We get bombarded every day with new health strategies, diet plans, power drinks, health bars, frozen low calorie meals, and vitamin supplements to get you in perfect fitness. Maybe it's best to follow what your body tells you, what feels right and what gets your desired results so that you can maximize your body's potential. Take the time and do some research to help you design your regular common sense healthy meals. Personally, I eat whole grain cereal almost every morning and I add strawberries, blueberries, walnuts, raisins, and coconut shavings. I regularly eat at least 3-5 vegetables every day. No alcohol, mostly water and a little soda pop, ginger ale. The only supplement I take is fish oil. Work on always improving your body's physical condition. You're either growing or decaying.

"A man's health can be judged by which he takes two at a time - pills or stairs." ~ Joan Welch

I exercise six days per week. At the gym or outside, I do endurance training, (usually at least 90 minutes of long distance running) speed intervals, stretching and weight lifting. Three years ago it was very apparent that I needed a basic change of lifestyle. That lifestyle now includes a rigorous exercise routine. Make it a priority or your train might stumble, sputter and spazz out.

Plan your weekly exercise routine on Sunday. What 50-90 minute activity will you do six days a week? And....rest. Yes, rest is very important. Give the body some time to recover after a strenuous workout. But if it's just a walk and you're not breaking a sweat, then you can do that everyday. Develop and maintain these healthy habits and you will not only arrive at your destination, you'll be 99 and feel like you're 32. You will feel better, look better and more importantly, you'll enjoy the trip.

MOTION CHANGES EMOTION

Moving means different things to different people. My mother used to say to brother Bradley, "you haven't moved a finger today." And then he'd raise his index finger up and down a few times and reply, " Yes I have, see?" We're talking "Jump-Start" action. Not the "run a marathon, climb Mt. McKinley" kind of movement. I mean action for the sole purpose of changing your feelings. The concept is simple. Use motion to change your emotion. If you're not feeling up to doing something that needs to be done (like working on a book you're writing) just start moving. For many people that may mean taking a walk to get the blood circulating, doing jumping jacks or push-ups. It might feel like it's the most impossible thing to do. My friend Jim used to say, take the action and the feeling will follow.

"Action seems to follow feeling, but really action and feeling go together; and by regulating the action, which is under more direct control of the will, we can indirectly regulate the feeling, which is not." ~ William James

It isn't about going to the gym for the cardio or weight training. It's about physically moving around to change your mood. Wipe those Dorito chips and cookie crumbs off your shirt, get off the couch and move your buttski!

Roger Johnson shared this story with me:

*One Monday morning I went into work in an awesome mood. The idea popped into my head that this day is "**High 5 Monday**". I walked up to our receptionist and greeted her with a huge smile, I said, "Good morning*

*Alice today is **High 5 Monday**." Then I raised my right hand and she took that cue to enthusiastically slap my hand and gave me back a beautiful smile. As I walked down the aisle between the cubicles, I approached all my sales team one by one and repeated what I had said to Alice, "Good morning _____, happy **High 5 Monday**." Each person slapped my hand accordingly and returned anywhere from a gigantic super smile to a reserved twinkle. Tuesday and Wednesday were a travel days for me so consequently I was not in the office. I went back on Thursday and repeated the same process with Alice and those in the office. That day it was **"High 5 Thursday"**. It really set the tone for a high energy and enthusiastic day. Two weeks later, I made it into the office at about 10:30 AM. I had hours of paper work to do. I sat at my computer and got down to work. A few minutes later, I heard someone from one of the cubicles say, "Hey, isn't today **High 5 Friday**?" I got up out of my chair and walked up to Larry and said, "Yes, it is. Thanks for re-minding me. Happy **High 5 Friday!**" And we gave each other very enthusiastic high fives.* The office energy rose to an 8 then a 9 and soon we were all on fire with 10+.

"It is remarkable how ones wits are sharpened by physical exercise." ~ Author Unknown

The point is this: To get the positive energy train back on track, it takes ACTION! Especially when we don't want to change our attitude. Maybe our old rusty train used to enjoy sitting in self-pity for a while, "poor me, poor me, I'm the victim, boo hoo." Now I Wake up and Shake Up! I take sustained action and my thoughts and feelings improve like magic. Do it. We have to break down that negative, lethargic feeling. Taking the "High

Five" action step is one way to get out of the blues. Remove Roger the Robber with intentional action.

"A body at rest tends to stay at rest. A body in motion tends to stay in motion." ~ Isaac Newton

FITNESS FUEL

What to eat, or what not to eat? That is the question. I still struggle a little bit with junk food. I am slowly getting better at eating healthy foods. We know we should eat our fruits, vegetables, and proteins. Here's a tip; Before you go to the grocery store make a list of fruits and veggies you normally like to eat. Then go online and look to see which vegetables you usually do not eat. Buy 'em and try 'em. It's good to vary the color of veggies you eat. So, eat some greens, yellows, reds, and purples. If that doesn't work, at least you've got some fun colors to look at. This train ride is about acquiring new success habits. Friends of mine are doing Jenny Craig, Weight Watchers and other well known plans. If one works for you, stick to it.

"When it comes to eating right and exercising, there is no 'I'll start tomorrow. Tomorrow is disease." ~ V.L. Allineare

MODEL YOUR MENTOR

Let's say you want to learn how to dance. What would be one of the first things you do? You might take a dance class which would be taught by an expert dancer. She knows dancing, loves dancing, and dances regularly. This person would model what to do. Make sense? If you kept at it, you would learn some pretty cool dance steps. She would be your coach. That is much more effective than reading a dance book and trying to learn to dance by looking at the diagrams.

"No man is capable of self-improvement if he sees no other model but himself." ~ Conrado I. Generoso

The same holds true for exercise and nutrition and basically almost all areas of your life. If you want to be a millionaire, it might be a good idea to associate with other millionaires. Now this might take a risk, but remember successful people do what unsuccessful people are not willing to do. Regarding your physical health, approach someone at your work, gym, or perhaps a neighbor who looks like he or she is in tip top physical shape. That means they look like they could play for the Boston Bruins or win the 2013 Ms. Pilates World Championship Award. You can tell. Ask what they do to stay in such tip top shape. Tell them you'd appreciate it if he or she would help you achieve your physical fitness goals. Three benefits you'll receive.

1. You've made a friend or strengthened a relationship.
2. You've made someone feel good by telling them you want to model their habits. (giving honest and sincere appreciation is huge)
3. You have a real role model who you can emulate in the area of physical fitness.

You don't have to adopt their fitness lifestyle today. Work into it slowly. But start making some changes. You can also hire a personal trainer. They make a living at getting people in lean, mean smooth running machine shape. You choose, but just get on track with your physical fitness. I strongly suggest you use a coach/mentor for other areas of your life where you want to see better results.

> *"A mentor is someone who sees more talent and ability within you, than you see in yourself, and helps bring it out of you." ~ Bob Proctor*

Meet people who are champions at what you want to do. Ask them how they got there. Then basically do what they did.

THE POWER OF CONNECTION

We know that there is strength in numbers. Ask your significant other, friend, neighbor or co-worker if they'd like to join you in some kind of fitness group program. Maybe three to five of you make it a point to go out for a 10 minute walk after lunch or on a break. This adds accountability, support and just more plain FUN. Move baby, MOVE! And remember teamwork gets better results in almost all areas of our lives. So join or start a pack and get on track.

> *"Teamwork is the ability to work together toward a common vision." ~ Andrew Carnegie*

BACK TO BASICS WITH BELIEFS

Let's go back to chapter 3 where we discussed how thinking and feeling what our clear intentions are, will lead to manifestation of those desires. Now we apply those thoughts, feelings and images to being in tip top physical shape. As with our GPS those vibrations, or feelings go out into the universe and attract similar vibrations. So let's say I visualize myself at my hunting weight...185 lbs. I imagine that I have a 32-inch waist and six pack abs. When I focus on those thoughts, images and good feelings about my physical condition, I attract circumstances, opportunities and situations like the following:

- I receive an unexpected check which is the same amount as a yearly membership to a nearby health club. Hmmmm, that's weird.
- A friend of mine says he's just started a new workout program and asks if I want to join him. Hmmm, that's even weirder.
- I somehow turn into the Trader Joe's parking lot instead of MacDonald's (no Happy Meals for you.) Guess it's time to eat healthy. Hmm, that's too weird.

"Hold a picture of yourself long and steadily enough in your mind's eye, and you will be drawn toward it." ~ Napoleon Hill

Now I still have to take the action. If I truly want to hit 185 lbs. a 32-inch waist and studley 6 pack abs I need to take the action. Yes, I am repeating myself ...take the action. It is action which matches your intention. Or sometimes called purposeful action. Now I can more clearly see the many opportunities available for me to do something healthier than I normally would have.

In conclusion, let's look at the topics we discussed in this chapter:

1. **TRAIN THE TRAIN**, start a 6 days per week exercise program
2. **MOTION CHANGES EMOTION,** get moving when you're feeling down

3. **FITNESS FUEL**, choose to eat the healthiest foods to give your train the right fuel (high test)
4. **MODEL YOUR MENTOR**, follow the advice of a mentor, coach or trainer to achieve similar results
5. **THE POWER OF CONNECTION**, exercising with family, friends and/or co-workers to have fun and get in shape while socializing. Power Packs on Track
6. **BACK TO BASICS WITH BELIEFS**, remember thoughts create feelings, feelings lead to our actions and our actions lead to results. So choose your thoughts wisely.

When the spiritual, mental and now the physical parts of our being are all functioning in harmony, we have a locomotive that is mean, lean and movin machine. And yet we still have two more very important principles which will add even more power to our train.

My train is making a U-turn...

"The first wealth is health." ~ Ralph Waldo Emerson

Back to the DEPOT

D.E. **P**.O.T. **P**hysical Health, how can you reach your maximum physical potential?

Chapter 5

DEP**O**T

Others come First

"I shall pass through this world but once. Any good therefore that I can do or any kindness that I can show to any human being, let me do it now. Let me not defer or neglect it, for I shall not pass this way again." ~
Mahatma Gandhi

A VERY NEW DIRECTION

Others? This isn't about other people is it? Isn't this a self-help book? Self; as in myself, me, yo, moi. I am trying to help myself. Duh... That's why I bought this book. Hello, McFly. Do-Re-Mi. Me, me, me. It's about me reaching my goals so I can have stuff. Cool stuff. Fun stuff. No? No. Well yes and no. Stay on board.

"An essential part of a happy, healthy life is being of service to others." ~ Sue Pattom Thoele

Oh you can acquire all that "stuff". No problema. But, and here's a "big butt"...IT'S NOT ABOUT YOU. I had a humongous challenge accepting this concept. It seemed to me that the happiest people were those with the coolest toys. Power, Prestige and Possessions were all that mattered. My train had to make a complete 180 degree turn regarding the whole way I looked at life. A friend of mine in my prayer group told me once, "Seth, there's only one thing you have to change to be happy...

73

and that's... EVERYTHING!" So much of what I believed for so many years, just wasn't true. Accepting this truth can take a while. I am still making slow progress in this area of my life. Sometimes I even take a step or two backwards. Who do I mostly think about? Me. Who is the most important person in the world? Me. Who should be served, revered and honored? Me, who else?

"The best way to find yourself is to lose yourself in the service of others." ~ Indira Gandhi

Arriving at your destination is important. More important is the growth we make and the person we become rather than the final arrival. And as we have discussed, we make "enjoying the journey" a priority. Remember you want to enjoy the ride. Believe that you will get there when you consistently take purposeful action. The end does not justify the means. The means justify the end. When you are peacefully, joyfully and enthusiastically riding your train, that's how your arrival will feel. Serving others helps bring you that peace, joy, and enthusiasm and then you'll have a happy and adventurous ride. If you are not enjoying the ride (feeling worried and stressed out) then, if and when you reach your destination, any satisfaction you experience will most likely be short-lived.

"Life's most persistent and urgent question is, 'what are you doing for others?' " ~ Martin Luther King Jr.

Let's do a quick recap. It goes like this:

1. We determine our destination/direction asking God for guidance (on a regular basis.)

2. We start each day with a 10 Xs Enthusiastic attitude
3. We keep our physical health in tip top shape, exercising and eating right. And now NUMERO KUATRO
4. We help "**O**ther people"

I finally came to believe in some universal principles which are designed to benefit all those involved, including me. One of these universal principles simply put goes like this: *"**You cannot receive what you don't give. Outflow determines inflow.**"--Eckhart Tolle* It's like your cup is running over. When you give to others your cup will be replenished. Trust in God and serve others. This is a principle which has a profound effect on my peace, joy and enthusiasm. Stay on board.

"You can get everything in life you want if you will just help enough other people get what they want" ~ Zig Ziglar

So there I was. Back in the late 90s I would regularly visit a men's jail in Orange County and speak about my challenging and yet joyful experience of turning my life and will over to the care of God. I had begun this new way of life about ten years earlier. The journey actually started on December 23, 1989. It has been awesome! Some ups and some downs, highs and lows, life "stuff", but basically Awesome.

Some of my more spiritual friends back then had suggested that I do some service work and pass my spiritual message on to others. This message is that since I started following my higher power's guidance, I have received a peace of mind, and a reassurance from God, that all is fine just the way it is right now. Reluctantly, I decided to be of service. About two to three times a month I drove to these county jails and spoke for about 40 to 50 minutes about my experience, strength and hope. Many of these inmates were there because they had committed a crime while they were under the influence of drugs and/or alcohol. The essence of my talk was that I had allowed God to come into my life and he had given me a purpose, a reason to live. My whole attitude and outlook on life has changed.

"You have not lived a perfect day, even though you have earned your money, unless you have done something for someone who will never be able to repay you." ~ Ruth Smeltzer

Our family owned a white Ford Explorer back then. I used to keep a couple of cigars handy in the glove compartment. On my way back home from the jail, I would light up a stogie and crank up the rock and roll. What a feeling of joy, exuberance and liveliness. My life was fantastic on that drive home. I was invincible, bulletproof and riding the wave of joy and excitement. If I had any problems, challenges, setbacks, or just all around downers in my life...they had disappeared. I was nicer to my wife and kids, the dogs and everyone around me. Yes, those current challenges would not solve themselves. But somehow they were minor inconveniences, not life threatening catastrophes.

"There is no exercise better for the heart than reaching down and lifting people up." ~ John Andrew Holmes

An improved attitude would allow me to see things from a different light. I felt a 'reassurance' that everything was going to work out just fine. I was more forgiving, and *more accepting of everything. How did this happen? All I did was give a talk to 30 men at a jail about turning my life over to God and the miraculous results I had received. It's one of the most important principles to assure success and happiness. When I help others, I am actually helping myself.*

"Life cannot make a selfish person happy." ~ TM

This was a new concept to me. When I give...I also receive. It may be strange, but it really works. Just like deciding to live life with 10 times more enthusiasm.

Here is a story from Chris P.

Presented with the opportunity to spend two weeks with a group from my church in Northern Uganda, I jumped at the chance. What an exciting adventure! But I very nearly pulled out of that trip just a few weeks after completing the interview. I debated whether I had signed up for purely selfish reasons. How could I, a thirty-something living in Southern California, possibly make a difference in a third-world country? What was my reason for going? I would show up for two weeks, only to leave and probably never return. A big part of our purpose in being there was to deliver medical assistance to the poorest villages in the African bush, and I had no medical training whatsoever. What did I have to offer these people? After some long talks with several people much wiser than I. I reconsidered and put my name back on the list. "This will change your life," one of the trip leaders

"Never worry about numbers. Help one person at a time, and always start with the person nearest you." ~ Mother Teresa

told me. And it did. Sure, I wasn't the medical expert in the group -- we had nurses and physicians assistants and EMTs for that. But I could help with the prep work, assist those more experienced than I, count pills for the prescriptions we were about to fill, and hold the hands of the Ugandan children as we treated them. It was amazing to see the hundreds of people lined up each day in hopes of being seen by a doctor or nurse. In some instances, the villages we visited hadn't received medical assistance in months -- and were desperately in need of it. At the end of each day, we rejoiced in the number of people in need that we were able to treat that day -- but were also left heartbroken knowing there were so many we didn't get to see.

"I find life an exciting business - and most exciting when it is lived for others." ~ Helen Keller

And that's when I had that "moment." It wasn't about me; it was about helping those in need. It is a very humbling experience to witness the need in a third-world country, and one's false pride and selfishness goes right out the door. Placed in a position where I had the opportunity to make a difference simply by making myself available to serve in whatever way possible, I found skills and talent and interests -- and joy -- that I never knew I had. Enough so that I would return just a few months later, helping to lead another group of people with many of those same doubts that I had. Yes, this changed my life.

Chris is a friend of mine from Toastmasters. Great guy. This trip changed his life. Some call it Karma, others call it the boomerang effect. Whatever you throw out or give to the universe, you will receive the essence of it in return. Give freely of yourself and know that you are on the right track. It brings an inner joy which is indescribable. Trust the process, expect miracles, have faith and believe, believe, believe.

> *"Give cheerfully and freely. It is the energy behind the giving that matters so do not give grudgingly. The law of cause and effect guarantees that you shall receive plenty for what you give." ~ David Cameron Gikandi*

THE REVERSE EFFECT

In the process of putting others first, there are two things to remember. First, when we help other people, we are actually helping ourselves. Even though we might not have the desired thinking or feeling to help someone else, we take the action first and then the right thinking and feeling will certainly follow. It's a good idea to follow what it says in 2 Corinthians 9:7- "God loves a cheerful giver." Am I a 24/7 cheerful giver? Well, not exactly. Occasionally I revert to my old way of thinking. Which is being selfish and self-centered. I am not a saint...believe me. Slowly, sometimes v e r y s l o w l y, I learn to put others first with a genuine smile on my face and a song in my heart. And then...peace. Ahhhh... the peace. Words cannot describe the peace. You'll have to experience it if you haven't already. And your train will run smoothly, gracefully and joyfully. Put others first and you'll get an "attitude of gratitude" (which is our next chapter).

The second thing to remember is that when you do little or nothing to help others or even worse, discourage others from achieving their goals, the universe, in the form of people and circumstances, will give you little if any help. It's like the stuff we were taught in kindergarden. Play well with others ...share. Ouch, sharing can be so hard. **Old Tracks:** Sharing is for losers, sissies, and not a good financial move. It's not a manly thing to do. **New Tracks:** I have learned that as far as "universal laws" are concerned, it is a good idea for me to accept them, obey them, and make them part of who I am. I will trust in God. He will help change this self-centered, selfish, egotistical toddler into a mature selfless, giving and mature man.

> *"In about the same degree as you are helpful, you will be happy." ~ Karl Reiland*

If this principle is going to help you be happy and successful and that is what you want, then just do it. Go help other people. You can acquire "stuff" and not even bat an eye at helping others. The problem is that "stuff" won't make you happy. It might for a short while but then you're left with you. And to be a "whole" person, we need to give of ourselves. I didn't write this universal law. I'm just telling you what I've learned on my train ride.

HAPPY AND USEFUL

I met a man back in 2008 at a prayer meeting in Orange County. His name is Bill. He was in his late 80s. Even though numerically speaking Bill was what many would consider an old-timer. Yet he had more energy, more zest and zeal than the Energizer bunny rabbit. He enthusiastically shook my hand and asked me how I was doing. He was very, very interested in my well-being. Bill made quite an impression on me. I wondered where he got the energy to run around like that, being of service everywhere he went? Bill was happy and useful.

"When you smile, your brain thinks you're happy." ~ Lia K.

Just a short time ago, I ran into a friend of Bill's. We briefly chatted and I remarked how amazing and inspiring Bill is. The other friend Jim, replied that Bill is now 90 years old. I shook my head and thought, wow, Bill is 90 and he has such a zest for life. Jim replied that his zest for life comes from helping others. That made me think. What a strange concept, happy and useful. When we put others first, not only does our attitude improve, but it positively affects our physical body. Now I don't know what Bill eats for breakfast, lunch and dinner. And I don't know his exercise routine. I guess he probably lives a very healthy life style, and maybe has for decades. When we add those healthy habits discussed in chapter four and mix it with putting others first....Watch Out!. Our engine becomes one fine tuned, revved up power-house machine that is virtually unstoppable. Bill is that example. That awesome example. That example that I want to follow. That I am following. Is there someone in your life who could serve as your role model? Hang out with him/her. Service and enthusiasm are contagious. Let's all be happy and useful!!!

Sounds hokey...pokey. And that's what it's all about. So here's the rub (finally got to use that line). We can find a plethora of quotes, stories and examples which show the personal benefits of putting others first. But where the train meets the track comes down to what you are presently and regularly doing to serve others? An important part of this step is to do it without telling anyone. Keep it to yourself. Otherwise, you're just feeding your ego, you want credit for that good turn. Remember practice makes permanent.

WHOM WILL YOU EMPOWER?

This is a simple assignment, an action step. As the title of this section states, choose someone to empower. It works like this. Take 24 hours to decide upon a person who you will do your best to empower. This could be a family member, friend, co-worker, neighbor or business associate. Do not tell anyone about this secret mission. Learn what his or her dreams, vision and goals are. Ask God to direct your thinking in the area of what is the best way to empower this individual. Then take that inspired action. Do it. No, really...DO IT!

EVERY CONVERSATION COUNTS

A friend told me that he does his best to make every single interaction he has with individuals Count (with a capital C). He once told me that any particular conversation you have throughout your day, may be an opportunity to hear a message from God. I used to think what my response was going to be while the person was still talking. When I am 100% attentive in my daily conversations, I'm amazed at how solutions to current challenges seem to appear. So make every single interaction you have with others COUNT.

"Listen first. Try to build bridges of understanding." ~ Dale Carnegie

82

Here's a quick review:

D: Know your **Direction**. Lead an intentional life.
E: Get **Enthusiastic** about your vision, your goals, and your journey.
P: Strive to achieve your top **Physical Health**
O: Helping **Others** is key to success
The last step to getting your life on track is.............
T: Maximizing the power of **Thankfulness**

This Success Express train ride is very cool...

"The value of a man should be seen in what he gives and not in what he is able to receive." ~ *Albert Einstein*

Back to the DEPOT

D.E.P.**O**.T. **O**thers come first. What are you doing on a regular basis to serve other people?

84

Chapter 6

DEPO **T**

T hankfulness

"Enjoy the little things in life, for one day you may look back and realize they were the big things."
~ **Author Unknown**

We talked about the power of enthusiasm earlier in chapter three. This last principle is also extremely Powerful. In fact many believe that the power of thankfulness, gratitude and appreciation is what is at the heart of making BIG CHANGES. Applying this principle is perhaps the key ingredient to having our train make a complete U-turn, not only turning our lives around and going in the right direction, but truckin on down the tracks with excitement, positive expectancy and 100% belief that we will arrive at our destination. Let's look at the power of being thankful.

"Gratitude is not only the greatest of virtues, but the parent of all others." ~ Cicero

As mentioned in the Enthusiasm chapter, when we allow negative input into our thinking, it can bring us down to a low energy, pessimistic, and unhealthy state of body and mind. Remember GIGO, Garbage In = Garbage Out. We want to quickly and habitually choose what thoughts to think. Even though we might feel discouraged, depressed, or even destroyed, when we refocus on those things in our lives for which we are thankful, our train can get back on track and power forward. It's not probable to feel 10 Xs ENTHUSIASTIC all the time. Sometimes, unfortunately Roger the Train Robber lurks in the sleeper car. He's that undercover, underhanded and sneaky sinister assassin. He wants to derail our train. DON'T LET HIM. Call in the TRAIN GANG. Remember the last "G" stands for Gratitude. The first part of the solution is to be aware that our train has this burglar on board. The difference is that now we have a sort of spiritual toolkit in our engineer's car that we can utilize to get our engine back in that lean, mean moving machine condition.

CAN YOU SEE THANKFULNESS IN OTHERS?

When we feel true thankfulness it shows on our face. A natural smile shines and can brighten up almost anyone's day. Charles Schwab said his smile was worth a million dollars. It helped him develop strong and long lasting relationships. James McConnell, a psychologist at the University of Michigan, said this about smiling, "People who smile, tend to manage, teach, and sell more effectively, and to raise happier children."

"The sexiest curve on your body is your smile." ~ Lia K.

How important is an attitude of gratitude? When we deepen and maintain this true feeling of thankfulness, we subsequently acquire the desire to share that good feeling with others. As we discussed before, our cup is running over. And as we give to others our cup will be replenished with more good feelings, positive situations and circumstances. It's a double win. More fire fuel for our train. Some call it serendipity, good luck, God shots or whatever. It's not that S_ _ _ Happens, Good Stuff Happens. We try to think of ways to help others and to show how much we appreciate them. Might it be inconvenient? Heck yeah. For me it is almost always inconvenient. It's fine to feel and talk about your appreciation; true appreciation must be acted upon. What do you do to show you are thankful? Be creative and do or give something unusual to show your appreciation. Let others know how much you appreciate them. Give honest personalized compliments. Remember it must be sincere, not flattery and not manipulation. Feelings follow action. Act and speak Thankful and you'll feel thankful. The chapter on "Others First" and this one are closely connected.

"Life can be seen through your eyes but it is not fully appreciated until it is seen through your heart." ~ Mary Xavier

I hadn't seen my friend Peter in six months, and the other day he was at our prayer meeting, wearing a smile from ear to ear. There was something difficult to define about him. About halfway through the meeting he shared some of what was happening in his life. The group listened quietly as he explained that his daughter was in jail awaiting trial, his wife was very ill and he did most of the care-giving. And the trifecta, he was getting laid off in two weeks. I thought about how I would deal with these overwhelming challenges. Would I have the patience and peace to just make it from one day to the next? My friend said, "This is the best day of my life." What? Did I hear him correctly? How could this be a good day?. "I'm in good health," my friend continued, "and I'll be seeing friends today for lunch that give me incredible support and encouragement." Well that stopped me dead in my tracks from blaming, making excuses and complaining. Here I was with all my family in excellent health, a job and no legal, or major financial problems whatsoever. I guess I got it pretty good, compared to Peter. And his attitude was amazing!

"Until I feared I would lose it, I never loved to read. One does not love breathing." ~ Harper Lee

On my drive home I made a mental list of all things I was grateful for. Here's what was on my gratitude list:

- I have a close personal relationship with God and he guides me, answers my prayers and strengthens me
- I am in outstanding health
- I eat delicious fresh fruits and vegetables every day
- I take calculated risks with courage and enthusiasm
- I'm alive...(that's better than the alternative)

My list continued to grow as I drove. I realized I had many reasons to be grateful. If my friend can be grateful when he's dealing with a trainload of challenges and tough times, I can certainly be grateful too. By creating a gratitude list on a regular basis, you can shift your perspective. New ideas, opportunities, and possibilities begin to open up. From these inspirational thoughts you can then take inspired action. These actions will help power your train so it runs like the Success Express it was meant to be.

"The single greatest thing you can do to change your life today would be to start being grateful for what you have right now. And the more grateful you are, the more you get." ~ Oprah Winfrey

Many happy people practice gratitude on a daily basis. That often helps put them in the right frame of mind. Instead of criticizing others, which is very easy to do, they look for ways to build people up.

Growing up, my mother would regularly try to make us feel thankful. She would tell us " The children in Cambodia don't know where their next meal is coming from. You kids should be grateful." My brother Bradley would reply, "they can have mine if they want." I am truly blessed. I have a roof over my head, and I am certain that today I will eat three delicious meals including fruits, vegetables and some form of protein. Millions of people do not even have that to look forward to.

Below is story about English Mike written by Lee R.

Attitude of Gratitude

In the late 1990's I was assigned to work on a project in a mid-size city in central Illinois. This was my first experience at living and working in this area and I was rewarded with meeting, working and socializing with what I thought were some of the most sincere and uncomplicated people I have been around.

One such person was a man everyone called "English Mike". I really don't know how he got that moniker but I recall someone saying he was originally from England and had migrated to the United States sometime after World War II. It was said that he was bestowed the highest military award given in the British Empire for his actions on D-Day on the beaches at Normandy. He never would talk about that and only mildly recognized that the story was true.

"English Mike" had become notable in this area of the country for his success in running a retail establishment.

Apparently his advertisements in papers and elsewhere drew attention to his store because of his outgoing and sometimes zany antics.

I met Mike at a fellowship I belonged to and immediately took a liking to him. One evening when I was with this group, English Mike showed up and said he had an announcement to make. We all listened as he began to tell us something that I will remember forever. Mike quietly said that earlier that day he had been told that he had terminal cancer and that his life expectancy would be counted in months not years. Those of us listening immediately reacted with dismay and sadness and it must have shown because Mike raised his voice and said we were not to worry, that he was fine with this discovery. He then told us why he felt so comfortable with this turn of events.

Over the years Mike had maintained what he called his "gratitude box". What this gratitude box consisted of was a shoebox with a hole cut in the top. Whenever he felt a feeling of gratitude for something that had happened to him he wrote it down on a small piece of paper and dropped it into the box. Over time the box was pretty full of these small gratitude notes. What he did with these notes was this: If something didn't go well or he was feeling out of sorts he would reach into the gratitude box and begin reading from those little notes. According to Mike it never took very long before he was out of his feeling blue mood and was remembering all that he was grateful for. He said it worked every time.

"We have no right to ask when a sorrow comes, 'Why did this happen to me?' unless we ask the same question for every joy that comes our way." ~ Author Unknown

That evening when Mike told us the sad news about his cancer he said the first thing he did was go from the doctor's office to his home, he pulled out the gratitude box and began reading. Then he came to our fellowship meeting and told us not only about his health problem but what he read from the little gratitude notes. He looked around at all of us and asked a simple question. He asked, how can anyone feel sorry for me when I have had so much in life and still have all those things and memories? The only thing that is different in his life now is that the end will be sooner rather than later.

For a couple of months Mike would show up at the fellowship, always beaming, always laughing, always grateful for the abundance of his life. It wasn't long afterwards that he stopped coming to the fellowship. He was now living in an assisted living home and was experiencing the inevitable deterioration of his health. I was able to visit Mike on a few occasions and he was always happy to see me and others who visited him as well. I never heard him complain of the situation he was in. He was more interested in what was going on with others than with his own plight. He would always talk about how good life has been.

Next to his bed was a shoe box with a hole in the top. He never shared what was in there but we knew it was filled with little notes that kept him forever in an attitude of gratitude.

He was missed by scores of admirers at his passing. The lesson he taught us has been invaluable to all who knew and embraced this gentle giant.

Those people who are grateful are happy, and those that aren't, aren't. Developing and maintaining an attitude of gratitude might very well be the most valuable action you can take when it comes to our train making a U-turn.

ACTION STEPS

Research at U.S. universities has revealed that there are six practices which will most effectively help develop and maintain an attitude of thankfulness. If done faithfully, you will have an attitude of gratitude in no time:

1. Keep a daily gratitude journal in which you make note of all the good things and the gifts that have come your way that day.

2. Promise yourself to practice gratitude regularly.

3. Focus on the good things that others have done for you. This makes us realize how interdependent we are and reminds us that we are loved.

4. Learn to develop a language of gratitude rather than a language of complaint. Ask your friends and family to help you. It's often hard to see for ourselves how much we're complaining.

5. Use your senses to come into the present and appreciate the small gifts in the moment: the smile of a child, the smell of your first cup of coffee in the morning, the beauty of a sunset.

6. Take grateful actions. Smile, perform random acts of kindness, help a stranger. Write a thank you card once a week and mail it.

Here's another idea on how to change your thinking. Try appreciating difficult situations and the biggie...try appreciating difficult people. There's a challenge. So when we encounter someone who is just downright mean, controlling and selfish, instead of getting upset at them and wishing they'd get hit by a train, be thankful. Be grateful that you now have an opportunity to practice love, compassion, and patience. There's another good book that says, "love thy neighbor". Talk about a U-turn!

"The struggle ends when the gratitude begins." ~ Neale Walsch

You can appreciate so many things in your life. It could be your toothpaste, strawberries, a cool beverage, clean air, clean chonies, the ocean, cookies, coffee, smart phones, breathing, a smile, perfume, ESPN, lactose free milk, rich robust coffee, chocolate. The list is endless.

You might have depressing debt or family and friends who are not in good health and maybe some dysfunctional relationships but, the truth is that there are plenty of people, places and things to appreciate. When you refocus your thoughts on "Thankful Things" you will actually attract the situations that you want to improve. You will find a way to get out of debt, connect with other Trains on Track Power People, calmly handle life's vicissitudes and enjoy the railway ride.

"As we express our gratitude, we must never forget that the highest appreciation is not to utter words, but to live by them."
~ John F. Kennedy

Back to the DEPOT

D.E.P.O.**T.** **T**hankfulness, how can you improve your attitude of gratitude?

Chapter 7
Success Express Summary

"The journey is the reward"
~ Chinese Proverb

ROCKIN ON THE RAILROAD

Congratulations! You made it. Or better yet, you're making it. As the quote above points out, there is no real destination. It's ALL about the adventurous, exciting and mysterious journey we are on. Enjoy the moment, energize your soul and embrace the mystery. Really understand that we are here in this physical body for such a short time. Why not make the most of it? Before you know it you'll be six feet under or perhaps sitting on someone's mantle above the big screen TV, and not a good view to watch ESPN from. Eventually, the train ride will end. That gives us one huge reason to live life to the fullest. Remember, you are the engineer. It's your choice as to what kind of train ride you're going to experience. A train ride that's magnificent or meager? A determined locomotive or a derailed train wreck? A powerful protagonist or a paralyzed pot of poop? As we review the DEPOT train tactics, there are three important concepts to remember: Growth, God and Go.

"Today is life – the only life you are sure of. Make the most of today." ~ Dale Carnegie

GROW, GROW, GROW

One of my mentors asked me what I would want my

children and grandchildren to say about me at my funeral. Would I want them to say, "he could have been a huge success, he had so much potential, if only he had persevered just a little more?" Or would I prefer them to say, " Wow? He gave it everything he had and didn't hold anything back, he had a dream and went for it, he lived life to the FULLEST! I think you know which words and feelings I'd rather have my children pass along to my funeral's attendees. What dream and vision are you pursuing that you might have previously thought was impossible? Get out of your comfort zone and at least start believing that you're making progress toward your dream? Take some kind of action today to move you closer to your destination.

"You must live in the present, launch yourself on every wave, find your eternity in each moment." ~ Henry David Thoreau

These train tracks can take you anywhere. SO THINK BIG, REAL BIG. Read this aloud: "I have grown and I'll continue to grow. I want to grow. I need to grow. My train may get jolted, side-tracked or Roger the Robber might slow me down. But I will NOT be stopped, I will not be deterred, I will NOT be derailed. I will do whatever it takes to make my train reach its destination." (good job) Many people like the "What doesn't kill me, makes me stronger" concept. Read the story below which reveals where I was a while back.

"Life isn't about waiting for the storm to pass. It's about learning to Dance in the Rain." ~ Author Unknown

So there I was in my statistics class at the University of New Haven. Each student would deliver a 10-15 minute presentation on a statistics project. I had chosen the topic of biorhythms. Created by German physician, Wilhelm Fliess. A biorhythm is the belief that the body goes through various cycles through time. I don't remember what specific content I had planned to present that doomful day, but I do remember a very cute Italian girl Gina, who I had a huge crush on. My plan was to completely impress Gina with my extraordinary public speaking skills, she'd fall in love with me and presto pesto we're visiting Rome, Venice and Florence over the upcoming holidays. That was Plan A. That didn't happen. I didn't have a Plan B. Ouch.

"If you voluntarily quit in the face of adversity, you'll wonder about it for the rest of your life." ~ Bill Clinton

I get up in front of the class with my flip chart and my 3 x 5 note cards. I'm getting ready, arranging my things. I turn around to face the class (about 20 students and the professor) and I FREEZE! That's right, frozen, deer in the headlights, with sweat pouring down my forehead. I saw the exit sign above the door to my right and the incessant thought of bolting, permeated my mushy mind. Do I make a break for it now? I gotta get outta here. This is TORTURE, SHEER TORTURE. The Italian girl is not going on a date with me, she's not vacationing in Rome with me, and I don't think she's going to marry me. Plan A, trash. Not a good day to be me.

Fast forward many years. I am delivering a 5-7 minute humorous speech dressed up as Robin Hood with a grey tunic, green tights, and a feather in my Robin Hood hat. I expressively spoke with an English accent and took second place in the final round of the contest. That is from the same guy who wanted to run out of that classroom not too long ago. Have I grown? I'd like to think so. Do I still have a tremendous fear of speaking in public? I now jump on board any opportunity to speak in front of five people or 5,000 people. I mostly go up on stage and have a blast. Yes, I get the butterflies before taking the stage. After a few minutes, they've gracefully flown away. I can relax, have fun and move to get on track, stay on track and not look back.

"The only way to get rid of the fear of doing something is to go out ... and do it." ~ Susan J.

The point is that I have GROWN. My self-confidence has grown a ton. My ability to develop and maintain healthy relationships has grown and number **1** on the priority list, my personal relationship with God has Grown.

Research shows that those people who make what is sometimes called a bucket list, wish list, life goals, or dream list and actually write them down, have a much higher probability of achieving those desires than those who don't. Your action step is make that list. In the reference part of this book there is a "bucket list" page. It's numbered 1-50. If you haven't done this yet, get a pen and start thinking, dreaming and writing.

GOD COMES FIRST

You're not alone. Focus on continuing to improve your conscious contact with God. As we discussed earlier, prayer and meditation are great tools to help us get closer to God. When you make God your top priority this I promise; you will be rocketed into the fourth dimension and guided by a power who wants you to enjoy your time here on Earth. Ask God in your morning prayer and meditation to guide you throughout the day. Talk to Him. Do it anywhere. I frequently turn off the car radio, CD player and just have a heart to heart conversation with Him. He knows what's going on in your life. He has a plan for you and a plan for me and all we need to do is basically get out of the way and let it unfold. Is that always easy? No way Jose. I still want my plans to happen now or better yet yesterday. One of my prayer group friends reminds me that God is more concerned about my character than my comfort.

"...whatever you ask for in prayer, believe that you have received it, and it will be yours." ~ Mark 11:24

His goal is not to pamper us but to perfect us spiritually. My friend Al told me that when he doesn't get any specific guidance from God regarding an important decision or action he remembers this: "when the student takes the test, the teacher is silent." We can figure things out with the brains He gave us. God is the director. He has everything under control. In God we trust. **TRUST IS HUGE**. I trust that God will work his miracles for what is best for me and guide me to a fulfilling life of peace and joy. He is the key to really enjoying your journey. He wants you to stay on track with him. This letting go and letting God, way of living can take years and years to develop. Remember me, the "rage-a-holic"? I had no patience, no peace and no joy. Like I said at the beginning of the book, I was a train wreck. My life sucked...big time. Now I take things one day at a time and trust that God will do for me what I cannot do for myself. Trust. and finally...

GO, GO, GO

As mentioned many times in this book, in order to enjoy the train ride and arrive at our destination, we need to take ACTION. Let's review.

- **D**: Does your **Direction** need more clarity and/or specific goals? Ask God for more clarity, seek input from those who have gone before you. Go and clearly determine what your dreams, vision and goals are. Follow your bliss.
- **E**: How can you improve your **Enthusiasm** level? Are you applying all of the "Engine, Engine Number 9" train tactics? Do them and trust the train...ing. Call in the Train Gang when needed.
- **P**: **Physical Health**. Persist on achieving tip-top. maximum body form. It's progress, not perfection. Are you getting fit, firm and ripped?
- **O**: How can you more regularly put **Others** first? How are you serving others? Are you making all interactions count? Practice random acts of kindness.
- **T**: Are you habitually thinking, feeling, and showing how **Thankful** you are? Revisit chapter six and redouble your efforts to be more grateful on a daily basis.

This is a five step process. Do your best to remember to go back to the **D E P O T** so you will enjoy the ride and arrive at your destination. If all these principles and ideas seem daunting to you, remember what Martin Luther King said, "Take the first step in faith. You don't have to see the whole staircase, just the first step."

Beginning is huge. Your train will start moving and you'll soon know you're living a life of intention, purpose and passion. Feelings of exhilaration, excitement and enthusiasm will come to dominate your daily emotions.

"Take time to deliberate; but when the time for action arrives, stop thinking and go in." ~ Napoleon Bonaparte

TRAIN TACTICS TO HABITS

When we apply and then live these five steps on a day-to-day basis, we can turn our lives around. Our train can and will make a U-turn. We have more control over our destiny than we think. We don't have to be wondering generalities. We can be like an arrow flying through the air knowing with 100% faith that we will hit the bull's-eye. So go for it. Don't hold back. Give it everything you've got. With God on our side and us doing the footwork, you will enjoy your train ride and reach your destination. That I know for sure.

"Neither a wise man nor a brave man lies down on the tracks of history to wait for the train of the future to run over him." ~ Dwight D. Eisenhower

CONTRARY ACTION

Some or perhaps all of these steps might not only be new behaviors to begin to apply, they might also go 180 degrees in the opposite direction from the way you've been doing things. Having your train make a U-turn might not happen in 30 days. Remember you have been conditioned with your limiting beliefs, harmful habits and a maladjusted mindset for many, many years. Get on the right track stay on track. Enjoy the ride. If you're like me, you want instant gratification. You might want the money and the perfect partner. I used to think that once those two biggies (finance and romance) were satisfied then I would be at peace with everything. God can bring you the peace you're searching for. Keep the faith.

"Don't ask yourself what the world needs.
Ask yourself what makes you come alive and
then go do that. Because what the world needs
is people who have come alive." ~ Dr. Howard Thurman

Sometimes it happens quickly and sometimes slowly. My U-turn has been a very slow **trains-formation**. One trick that I often use is to do the action which is contrary to what my first thought might be. Frequently, my first thought is to feed my ego. It is based on me being a selfish and self-centered egomaniac and acting like a two-year old. I seldom revert to toddler Sethy, but I do slip on occasion. Solution: I take contrary action and do the opposite of that. Change can be difficult. This is one of the biggest miracles EVER! We can change. You can change. Some of you will take the action and see huge results. Others will keep the knowledge in their minds but not act on these train tactics. How badly do you want change?

These tactics work whether you are changing a sour attitude you've had for the last 31 years or if it's a bad attitude you got ten seconds ago. It's about changing the direction of our thoughts and feelings from negative to positive. Believe your train can and will make a U-turn.

"Create a definite plan for carrying out your desire and
begin at once, whether you are ready or not, put this plan into
action." ~ Napoleon Hill

When you whole heartily apply these tactics you'll achieve a Passion for life. And I mean a HUGE PASSION!!! My personal relationship with God is the most important thing in my life. He allows U-turns. After growing my Faith in God, the First Five things I am most passionate about are the following:

1. My relationships with my children
2. Striving for tip top physical health
3. Inspiring others to do their best, be their best and live and work with (10) times more Enthusiasm
4. Engaging in a fulfilling relationships with family, friends and my significant other
5. Enjoying life to the fullest with fun activities like travel, sports, games and other entertaining events

Your train will make a U-turn and you live your life with joy, adventure and enthusiasm. You now have the tools to help you take the most exciting ride in the world-- your ride on the **Success Express**. Jump on board, stay on track and I'll see you at the Dynamic DEPOT! And remember,

Trains Make U-turns!!!

The closing caboose quotes are...

"Twenty years from now you will be more disappointed by the things you didn't do than by the ones you did do. So throw off the bowlines. Sail away from the safe harbor. Catch the trade winds in your sails. Explore. Dream. Discover." ~ Mark Twain

"Life should NOT be a journey to the grave with the intention of arriving safely in an attractive and well preserved body, but rather to skid in sideways, chocolate in one hand, Perrier in the other, body thoroughly used up, totally worn out and screaming "WOO HOO what a ride!" ~ Anonymous

D irection

E nthusiasm

P hysical Health

O thers First

T hankfulness

References, forms and readings

Suggested Reading List: There are so many good books out there to read. These are ones that continue to help me make significant growth.
Bucket List: Take some time to make the list and then go for it. Just do it.
Appreciation List: This ties in with the "T" chapter on Thankfulness. Very powerful stuff.
Scriptures to Strengthen Your Faith: I read these on my lunch break and then meditate for 10 minutes

Suggested Reading

- WORDS TO LIVE BY - Eknath Easwaran
- A NEW EARTH - Eckhart Tolle
- MONEY AND THE LAW OF ATTRACTION - Esther Hicks
- SECRETS OF THE MILLIONAIRE MIND - T. Harv Eker
- UNTETHERED SOUL - Michael Singer
- YOUNGER NEXT YEAR - Chris Crowley & Henry S. Lodge
- THE MAGIC OF THINKING BIG - David Schwartz
- RICHES WITHIN YOUR REACH - Robert Collier
- THINK AND GROW RICH - Napoleon Hill
- HOW TO WIN FRIENDS AND INFLUENCE PEOPLE - Dale Carnegie
- THE BIBLE
- CORAZÓN DE MUJER - Sheryl Roush
- THE ALCHEMIST - Paulo Coelho
- THE LITTLE ENGINE THAT COULD - Watty Piper

The Bucket List

Make a list of 50 things you would like to achieve or experience. Be ADVENTUROUS!!!

1. _____
2. _____
3. _____
4. _____
5. _____
6. _____
7. _____
8. _____
9. _____
10. _____
11. _____
12. _____
13. _____
14. _____
15. _____
16. _____
17. _____
18. _____
19. _____
20. _____

21.＿＿＿＿＿＿＿＿＿＿＿＿＿＿＿＿＿＿＿＿＿＿

22.＿＿＿＿＿＿＿＿＿＿＿＿＿＿＿＿＿＿＿＿＿＿

23.＿＿＿＿＿＿＿＿＿＿＿＿＿＿＿＿＿＿＿＿＿＿

24.＿＿＿＿＿＿＿＿＿＿＿＿＿＿＿＿＿＿＿＿＿＿

25.＿＿＿＿＿＿＿＿＿＿＿＿＿＿＿＿＿＿＿＿＿＿

26.＿＿＿＿＿＿＿＿＿＿＿＿＿＿＿＿＿＿＿＿＿＿

27.＿＿＿＿＿＿＿＿＿＿＿＿＿＿＿＿＿＿＿＿＿＿

28.＿＿＿＿＿＿＿＿＿＿＿＿＿＿＿＿＿＿＿＿＿＿

29.＿＿＿＿＿＿＿＿＿＿＿＿＿＿＿＿＿＿＿＿＿＿

30.＿＿＿＿＿＿＿＿＿＿＿＿＿＿＿＿＿＿＿＿＿＿

31.＿＿＿＿＿＿＿＿＿＿＿＿＿＿＿＿＿＿＿＿＿＿

32.＿＿＿＿＿＿＿＿＿＿＿＿＿＿＿＿＿＿＿＿＿＿

33.＿＿＿＿＿＿＿＿＿＿＿＿＿＿＿＿＿＿＿＿＿＿

34.＿＿＿＿＿＿＿＿＿＿＿＿＿＿＿＿＿＿＿＿＿＿

35.＿＿＿＿＿＿＿＿＿＿＿＿＿＿＿＿＿＿＿＿＿＿

36.＿＿＿＿＿＿＿＿＿＿＿＿＿＿＿＿＿＿＿＿＿＿

37.＿＿＿＿＿＿＿＿＿＿＿＿＿＿＿＿＿＿＿＿＿＿

38.＿＿＿＿＿＿＿＿＿＿＿＿＿＿＿＿＿＿＿＿＿＿

39.＿＿＿＿＿＿＿＿＿＿＿＿＿＿＿＿＿＿＿＿＿＿

40.＿＿＿＿＿＿＿＿＿＿＿＿＿＿＿＿＿＿＿＿＿＿

41.＿＿＿＿＿＿＿＿＿＿＿＿＿＿＿＿＿＿＿＿＿＿

42.＿＿＿＿＿＿＿＿＿＿＿＿＿＿＿＿＿＿＿＿＿＿

43.＿＿＿＿＿＿＿＿＿＿＿＿＿＿＿＿＿＿＿＿＿＿

44._____

45._____

46._____

47._____

48._____

49._____

50._____

The Thankful List

Make a list of the top ten things you are thankful for:

1. _____

2. _____

3. _____

4. _____

5. _____

6. _____

7. _____

8. _____

9. _____

10. _____

Scriptures to Strengthen Your Faith

1 Peter 5:7

Let Him have all your worries and cares, for He is always thinking about you and watching everything that concerns you.

John 14:27

I am leaving you with a gift - peace of mind and heart! And the peace I give isn't fragile like the peace the world gives. So don't be troubled or afraid.

Philippians 4:6-7

Don't worry about anything; instead, pray about everything; tell God your needs, and don't forget to thank Him for His answers. If you do this, you will experience God's peace, which is far more wonderful than the human mind can understand.

Psalms 40:1-3

I waited patiently for God to help me; then He listened and heard my cry. He lifted me out of the pit of despair, out from the bog and the mire, and set my feet on a hard, firm path and steadied me as I walked along. He has given me a new song to sing, of praises to our God. Now many will hear of the glorious things He did for me, and stand in awe before the Lord, and put their trust in Him.

James 5:7-8

Now as for you, dear brothers who are waiting for the Lord's return, be patient, like a farmer who waits until the autumn for his precious harvest to ripen. Yes, be patient. And take courage, for the coming of the Lord is near.

Romans 8:24-25

We are saved by trusting. And trusting means looking forward to getting something we don't yet have - for a man who already has something doesn't need to hope and trust that he will get it. But if we must keep trusting God for something that hasn't happened yet, it teaches us to wait patiently and confidently.

James 1:2-4

Dear brothers, is your life full of difficulties and temptations? Then be happy, for when the way is rough, your patience has a chance to grow. So let it grow, and don't try to squirm out of your problems. For when your patience is finally in full bloom, then you will be ready for anything; strong in character, full and complete.

Disclaimer

Acknowledgements

There were many people who helped me write this book. Firstly, a huge thanks to Franklin and Melinda, my children. They would frequently ask me how the book was coming along. Secondly, thank you to my ex-wife Delia. She had tremendous patience during this very long endeavor.

After working on this book for about two years and getting side tracked and off track, I met two beautiful, intelligent and very funny women, Annette Evans and Louise Hyland. We became very close friends and had train-loads of fun every week at our writers' group meeting. And yes, we did actually get some work done. Thank you Annette and Louise for the great times.

Made in the USA
San Bernardino, CA
12 October 2016